My Angel

Was The

Cable Guy

Lynne White Poole

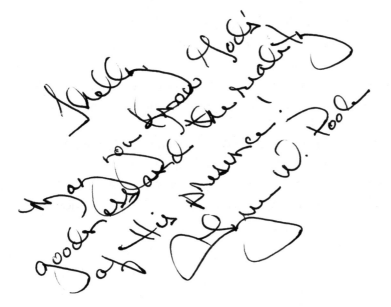

This book is a beautiful and powerful story of God's goodness and faithfulness. Your life will be transformed as you experience how God guided and walked closely with Lynne throughout her life!

Allison Carwile Wilson
Friend, author, and career coach

The Holy Spirit has used Lynne's lifetime faithful journey with our Lord as a testament that God is with us always. I felt such peace and love while reading My Angel was the Cable Guy.

Suzanne Landsverk

You hear Lynne's voice throughout this story, but more importantly you hear the voice of God in this story of life. You will laugh, smile, cry and praise God as you read each page.

Carol Cooley
Owner of CLC Consulting.

This history of one redeemed persons walk through trials and hardships, victories and disappointments with an eternal perspective will be an inspiration for all readers, but especially for those experiencing similar difficulties along life's journey.

Joyce and David Howell
Sunday school teacher of young children for 35 years and still greatly involved in spreading the Good News of Jesus Christ

The author tells a powerful and consuming life testimony that compels the reader to be grateful for every day, to value life, and to realize that our destiny is controlled by the Lord.

Each life disaster and gift molded the author and strengthened Lynne and her family's faith. The care of a special child strengthened her faith and enabled her to better share experiences and to teach. This book illustrates the reality of Scripture and its potential to guide our lives and open our minds to spiritual truth.

Symbols and angels along with the Lord's directional guidance fill the pages. The truth and lessons from God are formative for us all. The value of spiritual support in loss and illness are undeniable. Eternity and the truth of the closeness of Heaven enable all of us to deal with life's adversities.

James D Bearden III, MD, FACP, CIP, VP Clinical Research SRHS
Contact PI Upstate Carolina NCORP
Associate Medical Director
Gibbs Cancer Center and Research Institute
SMC-Center for Hematology/Oncology

Cover design by Krystine Kercher

Cover art: Angel at the Door, painting by Becky Wise, 2020; used by permission; Spartanburg, SC

Cardinal — Stock Vector Image, photo by Mikhaylova 2015; used by permission of DepositPhotos; Krasnogorsk, Russian Federation.

My Angel Was The Cable Guy
By Lynne White Poole

ISBN: 978-1-952369-63-6

Published by EA Books Publishing, a division of
Living Parables of Central Florida, Inc. a 501c3

EABooksPublishing.com

Table of Contents

About the Author

Lynne White Poole is a native South Carolinian having grown up in Columbia and raised her family in Spartanburg. She and her husband, John, have been married for 41 years. They raised two boys and are now the proud grandparents of a granddaughter. Lynne took care of their oldest son, Lee, who had profound disabilities. Throughout Lee's life, she worked as an advocate for individuals with disabilities and was involved in creating new programs for adults with disabilities who were considered medically fragile. Always involved in her community and active in their sons' lives, she now enjoys retirement with her husband on the lake. Lynne and John are members at Westminster Presbyterian Church.

Email Lynne at l.poole@myangelwasthecableguy.com

Dedicated to
My Three Boys
And
My Two Girls

Acknowledgments

I want to take this opportunity to thank those who have held my hand as I ventured into this unknown path of writing a book. God said He had an amazing plan for my life. Never did I expect that I would write a book. I couldn't possibly know how God would bring my life experiences, walking hand in hand with Him, to this place.

Linda Gilden was my editor and patiently helped me bring this book to fruition. She was kind and thoughtful to someone who had no idea what she was doing. God brought Linda into my path and I was so grateful for her encouragement, support, suggestions and direction all along the way. Because of you, it is a much better book.

Becky Wise created the beautiful cover. She took my ideas and painted them to perfection. Thank you for your part in this book to captivate people's attention from the beginning.

A big thank you goes to my proofreaders for their time and willingness to peruse the book with their corrections and suggestions. It took all of us to get this book ready for publishing.

When our internet went down because a hurricane came through and made the power lines look like spaghetti, our son, Brad, helped me work through the task of getting the manuscript to the publisher. Not easy with a mom who knows just enough about computers to write, but not much else. Bless him for his patience of guiding me over the phone. Not an easy task. I appreciated Brad and Jenna's love and support.

John, my husband, was so supportive and encouraging through this process. He was patient over all the months of writing at my desk in the basement. When I would get frustrated, he would calm me down and get me refocused. When obstacles kept getting in the way, he was as determined as me to see the book to completion. He has walked most of this life journey with me. During the wonderful times and the darkest of times, we have stood side by side. After all these years, I love him more today than when we started this life together.

And most importantly, I want to thank my Lord and Savior Jesus Christ who was always near to me through all the years. I am grateful to the Holy Spirit for helping to bring my life to the pages of this book, to proclaim the deeds of God. I, also, want to thank Him for sending my angel, the cable guy, at a time when I needed comfort, encouragement and assurance. This experience was one of the most amazing moments in my life. May this book bring God all the glory!

Lynne Poole

Foreword

This is my journey, but it is God's story. Through the years, my life weaved together for His glory! I believe we are all given a story to tell – to tell the world about Jesus and His love for us. Through difficult times God will reveal Himself to us in ways we cannot imagine. He will display His grace and mercy. He will comfort and heal us according to His will. This is His unfolding perfect plan, given for His purpose, for my life.

David proclaims in The Psalms that we are to declare the deeds of God!

> "Yet I am always with you;
> You hold me by my right hand.
> You guide me with your counsel,
> and afterward you will take me into glory.
> Whom have I in heaven but you?
> and earth has nothing I desire besides you.
> My flesh and my heart may fail,
> but God is the strength of my heart
> and my portion forever.
> Those who are far from you will perish;
> You destroy all who are unfaithful to you.
> But as for me, it is good to be near God.
> I have made the Sovereign LORD my refuge;
> I will tell of all your deeds."
>
> Psalm 73:23-28

I want to share God's astounding deeds in my life. To be truthful, I want to shout from the mountain tops the things I have seen and heard from God. The reality of His presence to those who believe Him! To those who seek to know Him through His Word! The wonder of His everlasting love! God said, "I am the Alpha and the Omega!" (Revelation 22:13) Climb into the presence of the living God and feel His peace. His peace that is breathtaking! It is past our understanding. He fills us with His inexpressible joy! Jesus invites us to enter into His joy through a relationship with Him. The joy of the Lord does not enter into us, but we into it! And His faithfulness that assures hope! God is a promise keeper! That is His nature! He is trustworthy and faithful!

"But as for me, it is good to be near God..." (Psalm 73:28)
"For we cannot help speaking about what we have seen and heard." (Acts 4: 20)

The Beginning

"My frame was not hidden from you when I was
made in the secret place. When I was woven together in the
depths of the earth, your eyes saw my unformed body.
All the days ordained for me were written in your book
before one of them came to be."
Psalm 139:15-16

I heard once that if we have endured great trials, we have the potential for great praise. I believe when we are born, according to God's
divine appointment, "all the days ordained for me were written in
your book before one of them came to be" (Psalm 139:16b).

As we look back through the years of our lives, we can pin point
those life-changing events. The first for me started in a wonderful little
Baptist church in Columbia, South Carolina. It was not a big church.
And it was not a tiny church either. In my memory, I see a brick building
with a white steeple. There were steps from the entrance of the church
to the parking lot where I sat and waited for my dad to pick me up after
Wednesday night service. I can still see the wooden pews and the beautiful stained glass windows, the baptismal pool with the velvet curtains
behind the choir loft and the pulpit. They are such vivid, sweet memories.

I grew up in a home atmosphere, which at times, could be described as chaotic and unstable. My mom was the sweetest, most loving person with the biggest heart. She would do anything for you. Dad loved us without question. But, because of circumstances in their lives, at times they struggled dealing with life. During those difficult times, church became my sanctuary. Bless them, they were both Christians and saw to it that I was in church on a regular basis. Church was a secure place where God surrounded me as a little girl. I still remember that tranquil feeling in that church. To recognize that feeling at such a young age, the Holy Spirit must have filled that church. Surely the Lord was in that place.

At the age of eight, I received Christ as my Lord and Savior. I know that sounds very young, but it was truly a transforming moment in my life. God knew I would need Him in the many years to follow and set my heart on Him. I was baptized on a Sunday night. I clearly recall feeling as if I was floating back to Mom and Dad sitting in the pews. It would be one of many supernatural events to occur in my life through the power of the Holy Spirit living in my heart.

This was the first time I felt God's presence. God had already started to build His foundation within me. Jesus was the rock on which that foundation was built! A firm foundation for when the storms would come. I would not be shaken. This was the beginning of my relationship with Jesus. The wonderful thing about our Lord is we can come to know Him as a small child or as a person ready to leave this world. His arms are always open to receive us.

This foundation started as a child and continues to this day to be built on the Word of God. I could not possibly have known how those sword drills would be used in the future. We sat with Bibles in our laps, waited to hear the Scripture announced, then quickly searched to see who could find the Scripture first. This was a wonderful way to become familiar with my Bible as a child. Memorizing the Books of the Bible during Vacation Bible School and receiving a plate with Jesus' face in the center for my accomplishment. I was so excited I had actually learned all the books of the Bible. As I get older, they don't seem to come to me as quickly.

At the time, I didn't appreciate the treasure of these verses and hymns stored in my heart, but they would serve me well in the years to come. Memorizing and reciting Scripture in front of the whole church, in Girls Auxiliary, rose to the forefront of mind years later. Singing the wonderful hymns resonated in my soul and the Holy Spirit sang over me at one of the most grievous times I would ever experience. And most especially, hearing the Word of God from the pulpit from thoughtful, compassionate pastors built on that firm foundation.

All these undergirded me during the darkest days of my life. They were hidden away in my heart for just the right moment. The Holy Spirit brought God's Word to my mind and memory making all things incredibly clear during times it would have been so easy to get lost in the chaos of life. The words of Scripture are alive and saturated with the power of God. God's Word was a balm to my soul. It gave me comfort when I was grieving. Hope when I needed it. Encouragement when times were difficult. When you experience God's love and power you cannot help but speak about these things. I believe God has entrusted me with the task of telling others about God's awesome deeds.

> *"Many, O Lord my God, are the wonders you have done. The things you planned for us no one can recount to you: were I to speak and tell of them, they would be too many to declare" (Psalm 40:5).*

Quite a Start

"I will instruct you and teach you in the way you should go;
I will counsel you and watch over you."
Psalm 32:8

A s I grew up and got busy with life, I hate to admit, I drifted from my first love. I still prayed and went to church occasionally. But, God was on the periphery. The things of this world had grabbed my attention. My sisters and I took dancing lessons from the time we were three years of age through high school. I loved to dance. Ballet and tap were my focus. That was my life for many years. Dancing gave us the ability to participate in different opportunities. I cheered all through high school. I participated in beauty pageants and once on a national level. I modeled in New York, nothing noteworthy, but still a wonderful adventure. God used these experiences to increase my confidence to stand before a group of people and speak and teach many years later. This world can easily seduce you and Satan will use any and all opportunities to draw you away from God. Thank goodness God has promised to those who believe Him that He will never forsake or leave us. These true words would have profound meaning for me.

"The Lord himself goes before you and will be with you; He will never leave you or forsake you. Do not be afraid; do not be discouraged" (Deuteronomy 31:6).

I went to college and had a great time. I was a cheerleader my first year and also, joined a sorority. I enjoyed my experience at college, probably a little too much. I guess that is the process of growing up and hopefully, maturing. I was blessed with three amazing roommates who were all Christians. God still had His hand on me. I was going my own way for the time being. I was still leaving God on the periphery.

I had prayed for a very long time for God to bring just the right person into my life. I met my husband, John, through a dear friend and we were married a year later. It was one of those instant connections. We met at the lake and never looked back. Interesting to note, God brought us back to live on a lake in our retirement. John and I both knew it was a God thing! We had a beautiful church wedding and started our life together. I was in love and beyond happy. John was working at a bank on Hilton Head Island. I had never heard of the island. Growing up, when we went to the beach, it was a little further north at Myrtle Beach. So, to be a newlywed and living in this paradise seemed like a dream. We built a new home and all seemed well in the world. I was living a life beyond my wildest imagination. John and I decided we were ready to start a family. Hilton Head was a resort and we weren't sure we wanted to raise a family there. So, John transferred with the bank to Greenville, South Carolina.

I had always felt from a very young age my purpose in life was to be a mom. I can't explain it other than that was what I felt in my heart. I did not want to be a career woman. My goal was to be the best wife I could be and the best mom I could be. Little did I know how God would use that desire on a path I doubt I would have chosen. Our life was about to be forever changed. And now came the next pivotal point in my life. We all have plans, but when God interrupts them, sometimes all we can do is trust Him.

John and I were blessed to conceive easily. I would not be blessed with easy pregnancies. We had moved to Greenville and were thrilled beyond words that we were expecting a precious baby. Lee Sterling Poole came into our lives three months prematurely. We had not started the nursery. We had not had a baby shower. We didn't even know how to get to the hospital by the quickest route. I had been having back pain and my doctors thought I had pulled something in my back. They prescribed a pain medicine. This would turn out to be a mistake. The medicine disoriented me. By the time I could make sense of the situation, I was in trouble, I was in full labor. I crawled from the den to our bedroom to waken John. By the time we reached the hospital, I was fully dilated. Only God kept us from having Lee in the car.

Lee was born at 2:49 a.m. on May 2, 1982. He weighed 3 lb. 2 ½ oz. He measured 15 ¼ inches long. He was the tiniest thing I had ever seen. He went immediately to Neo-Natal Intensive Care Unit (NICU). The first time I was able to hold Lee was Mother's Day. The nurses wrapped him in three or four blankets so he wouldn't slip through my arms. He was on oxygen and doing well and then everything went bad on his second day. He had a massive intracranial bleed; his lungs collapsed; his heart stopped. He lay at deaths door for days. Those days were so painful the memory still makes me cry.

That beautiful plan for my life took a turn we could not have expected. We almost lost Lee that night. John and I stood at the foot of his bed praying to God to let us keep him. We promised we would do all we could to see that he had a healthy and happy life. We had no idea how we would need God in the years ahead to help fulfill that promise. I wrote on a yellow legal pad right after Lee's birth and placed it on our refrigerator: Miracles do happen! Never give up!

This precious child that God had brought into our lives transformed our lives and strengthened our faith. I have to admit I questioned God. I had tried to live right and be a "good person." Though I was never angry at God for this detour in our lives, I still had questions. Why? It would take time to see the blessings Lee would bring to us. It took much longer to understand God's perfect plan for Lee and our family. God had a much bigger plan for my life than in my limited vision. I would grow to trust God and come to a place of contentment and thankfulness. It was God's plan and His timing. I had to learn to wait on Him.

This fragile baby had many difficult times in the NICU. Lee dropped down to 2 lb. 3 oz. Scary tiny! He would be the first baby in Greenville to have a procedure to externally drain the fluid off his brain. With the trauma to the brain after the bleed, the nurses looked for signs like sucking for feeding. Praise God, he did suck. We had something to hang on to in those early days of the unknown. Lee was a fighter and survived many difficult challenges.

He was my baby and I already loved him more than I knew possible. While in the incubator, John and I played music to him and talked to him. We read to him, caressed him and prayed and prayed and prayed. After six weeks and what seemed like an eternity of having to leave my baby every evening, we were finally given the word we could take him home. I don't know if it was just sheer joy of bringing Lee home or ignorance or God giving me wisdom beyond my ability, but I couldn't wait to have him home in his crib so I could take care of him. No thought to what the future might hold.

Each day brought its own set of circumstances. As Lee grew, we came to understand the medical issues we would learn to navigate. Lee was declared blind, although we believed he saw light. He became hydrocephalic and needed a shunt to drain the cerebral fluid from his brain. Lee had cerebral palsy and would never sit or walk. He developed seizures when he was about three years old. Twice he stopped breathing and we had to call 911. With medication, a lot of patience and a great pediatrician, we were able to control many of the grand mal seizures. But, seizures became a part of our days. Lee became our barometer! We knew the weather was going to change before the weatherman. When it changed drastically, it seemed the pressure changed in his head and Lee had a seizure.

Because Lee was considered so medically fragile, the doctors wanted us to have another baby. They were concerned Lee would only live to be about a year old. God had different plans. John and I discussed and prayed about having another baby so quickly and decided to let the Lord make that decision for us.

And the Lord decided to bless us with another baby. We became pregnant. John took a position with the bank in Spartanburg. We had, also, looked at a position in Charlotte. We felt the best school for Lee was in Spartanburg. We had just moved into our new home and I was put to bed because of problems with my pregnancy. John had a new job, a baby with medical issues and a new house with things still in boxes. Now, he had a wife placed on total bedrest. Our neighbors had keys to our home throughout the neighborhood in case I had problems so someone could let EMS in the house. We were total strangers and yet, they kept watch over us. God carried us through those uncertain days. One day at a time! Looking back, that's the only way we made it.

It was December 31, 1983. We had gone through Thanksgiving and Christmas. Our Christmas tree was in our bedroom and stockings were hung on our closet doors. We had made it to the seventh week. Every day was another day for Brad to grow. The temperature had plummeted that night to below zero breaking records. John was watching a football game and I had fallen asleep. I awoke and knew instinctively something was wrong. I looked down and I had started hemorrhaging. I woke John and told him we needed to go to the hospital. When he saw I was bleeding, all the color drained from his face. I told him to grab a towel to put between my legs and to call a neighbor. The neighbor came immediately. His wife took Lee home with her until my parents could arrive. They wrapped me in blankets and carried me down the stairs to the front door into the cold night. When we arrived at the emergency room, they put me on a gurney and wheeled me to labor and delivery. Our sweet neighbor had not taken time to change and was in his pajamas and robe. He stayed to hear word in the waiting area. He said the nurses kept coming up to him and telling him he needed to go to his room. Bless his heart. He got us to the hospital and still in his pajamas.

I was praying the Lord would give us more time. Brad needed more time before coming into this world. It was New Year's Eve and I was praying Brad would not be the first born in 1984. They gave me a

9

blood transfusion and started steroid shots to help Brad's lungs. Since we had only lived in Spartanburg a couple of months, my doctors were in Greenville, 30 minutes away. The bleeding stopped and we waited to see if we avoided an early delivery. John said the phone lines were hot between Spartanburg and Greenville that night. The doctor on call went to school with my obstetrician. God still had His hand on us. The doctor knew my history of delivering early with Lee. He was not feeling well, but slept all night in the labor room next to mine. We made it through the night.

The next day they wheeled me to a regular room. That night I started having contractions. I received another shot of steroids to help Brad's lungs and was wheeled back to a labor room. Again, the contractions stopped and they watched me all night. The next morning I was wheeled back to a regular room.

John wanted to know if I wanted him to bring me some dinner. I was craving a hamburger. So in he walks with a hamburger, fries, and milk shake. I had hardly finished eating when the contractions started again. Back to the labor room we went. I looked up at John and said this is our third time headed to labor and delivery. I felt Brad was going to be born. God gave us enough time to get all three steroid shots to help his lungs. This would give him every opportunity to come out of NICU well.

I was having contractions, but had not dilated. They were concerned I was bleeding internally and decided to do an emergency caesarean section. Ready or not, Brad was coming into the world. I am not sure if I was going into shock or just scared, but I started shaking. A kind nurse leaned over me and said sweet words to comfort me. That's the last I remember. Because I had just eaten, they put me to sleep quickly and brought me out quickly to prevent me from aspirating.

For the second time, I had a new baby that was whisked away and I didn't get to see or hold either of them when they were born. Patrick Bradford Poole was born on the evening of January 2, 1984. God had blessed us with another son.

Lee was 18 months old and Brad was born two months prematurely. I can't begin to tell you how overwhelmed I was having a child with an uncertain future and now, a newborn, and a preemie no less. I believe it was the fear of the unknown. Lee had spent six weeks in NICU. He had one surgery before he left the hospital and two major surgeries before he was one. Was Brad going to be fine? Could I handle two tiny babies? But once we brought Brad home from the hospital two weeks later, I was all in and the family I had dreamed about was complete. I loved my boys with a deep, profound love. Not unlike all mothers. But, we had to endure a lot to get these babies. I did not take that for granted. I knew how blessed we were.

Brad did well after birth and brought normalcy to our lives. John and I truly delighted in every minute of our two sons. We had come to know how fragile life could be, yet we were so thankful. We were learning to live life one day at a time. There would be days ahead where we lived from moment to moment. This would be our journey of faith; faith to observe God's hand in absolutely everything.

"I can do everything through him who gives me strength"
(Philippians 4:13).

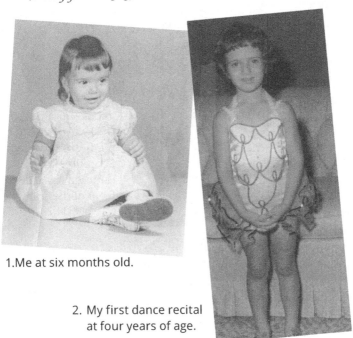

1.Me at six months old.

2. My first dance recital
at four years of age.

3. Robin, me and Cindy when I was about 10 years old. We were all involved in dance.

4. 1969 Girls Auxiliary in our church. I reached the level of queen by memorizing certain Scripture. It was required to recite in front of the church.

5. Dancing in Pas de Quatre 1971. At this time, dance was a large part of my life.

6. Cheering for the University of South Carolina 1975.

7. John and I were married on August 25, 1979 at Riverland Hills Baptist Church, Columbia, South Carolina.

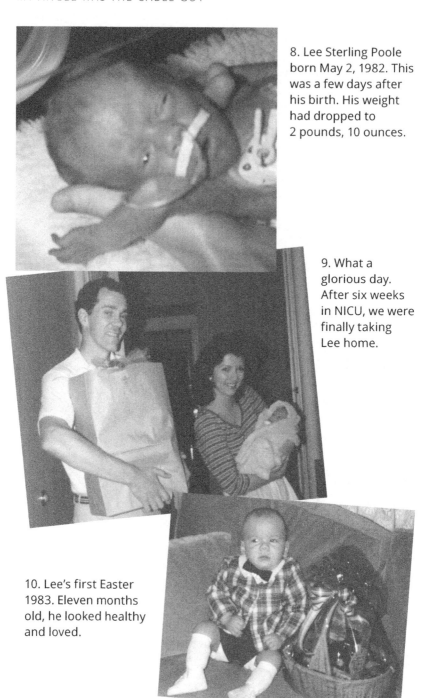

8. Lee Sterling Poole born May 2, 1982. This was a few days after his birth. His weight had dropped to 2 pounds, 10 ounces.

9. What a glorious day. After six weeks in NICU, we were finally taking Lee home.

10. Lee's first Easter 1983. Eleven months old, he looked healthy and loved.

11. This was shortly before Brad was born. In total bedrest, John took on the enormous task of caring for Lee, me, our home and working.

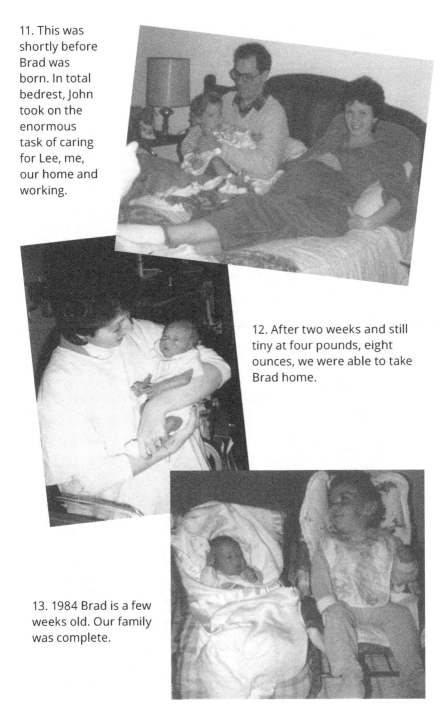

12. After two weeks and still tiny at four pounds, eight ounces, we were able to take Brad home.

13. 1984 Brad is a few weeks old. Our family was complete.

14. This was my father-in-law's, Lamar Poole, favorite picture. I was beyond happy. Brad, me and Lee.

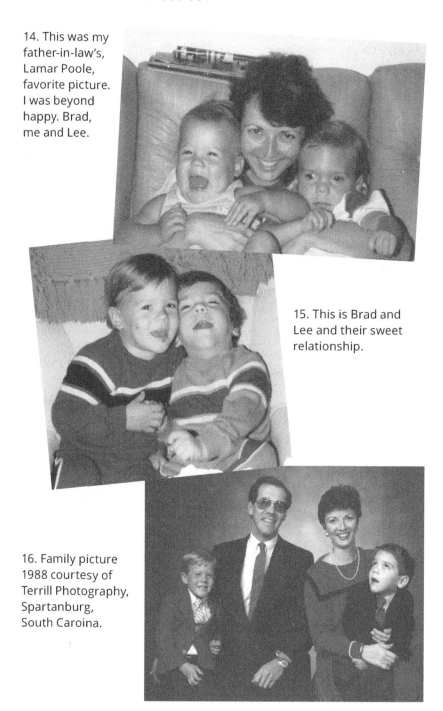

15. This is Brad and Lee and their sweet relationship.

16. Family picture 1988 courtesy of Terrill Photography, Spartanburg, South Caroina.

THREE

Gift's From Heaven

"There is a time for everything, and a season for every
activity under heaven: a time to be born and a time to die,
a time to plant and a time to uproot,"
Ecclesiastes 3: 1-2

Scripture tells us there is a time for everything, and God promises that our days will be beautiful in His unfolding, perfect plan. John and I had survived two extremely difficult pregnancies and were now parents of two precious boys. We were thrilled, but the first couple of years were like being thrown in the deep end of the pool with few swimming skills. It was like having twins. There were two bottles to feed, two in diapers and just two of everything. I remember the day Brad held his own bottle. I was beyond ecstatic!

Brad was the perfect baby. He went to bed smiling and he woke up smiling. He was happy all the time. I just adored him and loved watching him grow and develop. I believe God knew Lee's care would be 24-7 and blessed us with this loving, happy child. As he and Lee grew they had a special bond. I can remember one day when I found Brad, as a toddler, playing and rolling on the carpet with Lee. My first inclination was to run and stop them. But Lee was thoroughly enjoying the physical activity, smiling and happy.

As a small child, Brad heard constantly to be gentle with Lee. But as a toddler, he just wanted to play. So, I let them develop their own play. Brad pretended he was the bus driver and Lee was a passenger. They found a way. Lee let him know when he was finished playing. There came a time when Brad realized he was getting corrected and Lee was not. He felt he was getting the short end of the stick as it were! So we improvised and I would fuss at Lee for no specific reason. Brad seemed satisfied they were now on a level playing field. We learned as we went along.

Lee had a sweet connection with Brad. They had a unique relationship. Brad became, in essence, the older brother and watched over Lee. He was very protective of him. And, because of Lee's needs, Brad became very compassionate toward others. In grammar school, his teachers were always telling me of something Brad had done that day to help a fellow student. This was just one of many blessings that came through Lee's life.

We fell into daily life as a busy family. Ours was not your normal situation. But we adapted and that became our normal. Lee had to have all his needs taken care of by others. The first half of his life was trying to get his delicate medical needs tweaked. We worked continuously to fit the pieces of this complicated puzzle together. With persistence and a wonderful group of doctors who cared for and about Lee, we were able, with three medications, to control his seizures to a point. Salt was added to his water to keep his sodium from dropping to dangerous levels. Sometimes I felt like a chemist. I knew to the exact amount that was given to Lee for his medical need and nutrition each day. I had to learn to feed with a feeding tube down his nose. These were skills I never dreamed I would need to learn. I pushed forward trusting God to guide me along the way. Then we had a feeding tube placed in his abdomen which was so much easier for all of us. Especially Lee!

> *"He tends his flock like a shepherd; He gathers the lambs in his arms and carries them close to his heart; he gently leads those that have young" (Isaiah 40:11).*

Through Lee's life, I learned to listen to God's instruction. He fine-tuned my hearing to His sweet voice within my spirit. Becoming aware of that voice was how I learned to care for Lee. Lee was non-verbal, which was a challenge trying to discern his needs and wants. I came to understand when we yield our lives to the Holy Spirit, we can do things way beyond our comfort zone. And caring for Lee and his needs were way beyond mine. Yet, I continued to press forward. This was for Lee's wellbeing.

> "The Lord said, 'Go out and stand on the mountain in the presence of the Lord, for the Lord is about to pass by.' Then a great and powerful wind tore the mountains apart and shattered the rocks before the Lord, but the Lord was not in the wind. After the wind there was an earthquake, but the Lord was not in the earthquake. After the earthquake came a fire, but the Lord was not in the fire. And after the fire came a gentle whisper" (1 Kings 19:11-12).

God carried me along showing me which way to go. He directed my steps in ways that still overwhelm me. My faith was strengthened with every twist and turn along our path. I knew God was holding my hand. I didn't truly appreciate it until years after Lee came into our lives. I tried to care for Lee with joy for every task no matter how difficult the situation. I knew Lee was very sensitive to my emotions and I wanted him to feel this wonderful joy. I wanted Lee to know he was loved.

I discovered the only place to find that kind of joy is not of this earth, but through Christ. When you have the joy of the Lord, you find true peace. This peace is not found in positive thinking or good feelings. It comes from knowing God is in control. He is a faithful God and will see you through. Many times we got to the other side of a difficult challenge. We looked back and saw how God provided. I was filled with the joy of the Lord every day. I knew He was near and I could trust Him. There is a great comfort in that knowledge.

"Rejoice in the Lord always. I will say it again. Rejoice! Let your gentleness be evident to all. The Lord is near. Do not be anxious about anything, but in everything, by prayer and petition, with thanksgiving, present your requests to God. And the peace of God, which transcends all understanding will guard your hearts and your minds in Christ Jesus" (Philippians 4:4-7).

During these challenging days, I drew closer and closer to God. And He gently whispered to me what I needed to hear. There were times when I desperately needed Him and He sent someone to help me or He directed my steps. This took years for me to know Lee and his needs. During this time I was learning to listen with intention to the Holy Spirits leading.

That is not to say I wouldn't have sleepless nights caring for Lee's needs or days of exhaustion. However, I prayed to the Lord and He calmed my soul. There were times of waiting to find answers for Lee's various medical needs. Patience is not a natural virtue for me, especially with my family. But, sometimes, all we can do is wait.

Lee started having seizures and was admitted to the hospital. This was a frequent occurrence the first half of Lee's life. A neurologist was sent to consult on Lee's condition. This doctor could only see the disabilities and medical issues Lee had. He couldn't see this gift God had given us. Never having met us before, he advised me that if Lee had an emergency, we should just let him pass away. I was devastated at his advice and this opinion! I couldn't believe his arrogance. I immediately called Lee's pediatrician and told him what this doctor said. We were blessed with the most caring pediatrician. He told me not to worry about making this decision. When or if the time came, we'd make it together. God would use Lee's life to bless so many throughout the years. This neurologist had intelligence, but not wisdom, especially, not God's wisdom.

"'For my thoughts are not your thoughts, neither are your ways my ways,' declares the Lord" (Isaiah 55:8).

"For the message of the cross is foolishness to those who are perishing, but to us who are being saved it is the power of God. For it is written: "'I will destroy the wisdom of the wise; the intelligence of the intelligent I will frustrate. 'Where is the wise man? Where is the scholar? Where is the philosopher of this age? Has not God made foolish the wisdom of the world? For since in the wisdom of God the world through its wisdom did not know him..."' (1 Corinthians 1:18-21b)

The time came when I told the doctors what the issues were Lee was dealing with and what I thought we needed to do to help him. They understood I knew Lee better than anyone and generally agreed with my suggestions or at least trusted my input. They were still Lee's doctors, but we became a team, a united front for him.

The Lord blessed us in extraordinary ways. He brought Cris, Lee's second mom, into our lives. Lee would become part of Cris' family and grow up with her three children. She is a remarkable person and was gifted in caring for children with special needs. It was her calling. Cris would care for Lee while John and I tried to participate in most of Brad's activities. It also gave me the opportunity to join John with his numerous board activities. Our lives would have been very different if not for Cris and her loving family. She was truly a blessing from God.

The years passed and before we knew it Lee turned 13 years old, a major milestone in his life considering the doctors initial prognosis. He was long and lanky like his dad and had a head full of beautiful, thick wavy hair. Everyone, at some point, had their fingers in his hair. Rubbing his head, which he loved, or just playing with those curls. When I picked him up from school, he usually had three shades of lipstick from kisses on his face

October 1997 brought another pivotal moment in my life. We had an extremely difficult year. John's mom passed away from lung cancer. His dad was hospitalized fearing he may have cancer. Thankfully, he did not. During this time, we were living in an apartment. We bought a house that was being renovated so we could care for Lee as he got older. We had our furniture in the basement of a local business. Our neighbors were near, but not next door. It was a very trying time. The apartment was small enough to clean quickly and that was a blessing. There was no yard to maintain for John. Our time and energy would be needed elsewhere.

Lee became very agitated. It was impossible to comfort him and he cried day and night. This went on for days. We took him to see his pediatrician and his neurologist. They were trying different things, but nothing was working. Then Lee became almost comatose. Both doctors feared Lee had had a stroke and told John and me to prepare for the strong chance that Lee might not survive. I was not prepared for this at all and was struggling to cope. John had even suggested I seek counseling to help me. It was almost unbearable to even contemplate.

One afternoon, I held Lee rocking him and praying to God through tears that if it truly was time for Lee to go be with Him, I would give Lee back. I knew He knew my anguish because He had given His Son for me. I knew He knew my breaking heart and I would not question His plan. Suddenly, a sensation like that of warm honey seemed to be flowing down from my head over my body. I knew in my heart the Holy Spirit had come over me in an incomprehensible way and a peace and calm I had never known took away my fear. It took a while to truly comprehend this event. I had never experienced anything like this before. It would be a powerful experience of God that would draw me even closer to Him. I was resting and trusting in God completely. Then, I read the following passage years later:

> *"So Samuel took the horn of oil and anointed him in the presence of his brothers, and from that day on the Spirit of the Lord came upon David in power..." (1 Samuel 16:13).*

I believe the Holy Spirit prompted me to call the doctor again and he encouraged the neurosurgeon to see Lee. It was decided to perform exploratory surgery. The surgeon determined his shunt had malfunctioned and needed replacing. The shunt was used to drain the fluid off Lee's brain. Because it was not working, pressure had built up in his head. Thankfully, Lee came out of surgery wide eyed and feeling better. From that point on, Lee never had to go back in the hospital. We were in and out of the hospital those first thirteen years! For the next fifteen years, Lee flourished and thrived.

"Weeping may remain for a night, but rejoicing comes in the morning" (Psalm 30:5b).

FOUR

God's Guiding Light

"Forget the former things; do not dwell on the past.
See, I am doing a new thing! Now it springs up; do you
not perceive it? I am making a way in the desert and
streams in the wasteland . . . (for) the people I formed
for myself that they may proclaim my praise."
Isaiah 43:18-19, 21

As King Solomon tells us in Ecclesiastes Chapter 3, there is a season for every activity under heaven. I love when Isaiah says, "I am making a way . . . " That is what the Lord does. There are peaks and valleys in life. The Lord makes a way. It may not be what we would choose, God sees the bigger picture. Time continues to roll on! As a family, we moved forward trusting the Lord for discernment and wisdom. We never lamented our situation. We just learned to live life in a different way. We never complained. That would not have been fair to Lee. To us and in God's eyes, he was perfect just the way he was. We looked past his disabilities and saw the gift he was from God.

We chose to celebrate what Lee could do and not dwell on what he was not able to do. And how we celebrated! If he smiled, we rejoiced.

If he had a good night, we celebrated. During the first half of his life, difficult, sleepless nights were the norm. Good nights were few and far between. But the second half of his life, the good nights became the norm and the nights we had very little sleep were rare.

Lee knew just how to get his way and had everyone wrapped around his little finger. This was just too much fun to watch and see how he could get his way. He loved eating whipped topping! He loved the movie "Cars." He also for some strange reason, loved wrestling. Lee loved for his Dad to race him through the house in his wheel-chair with me yelling the whole time to be careful. He adored his brother. His face lit up when he heard Brad's voice. We threw our-selves into the moment. It's amazing how sweet life can be when you treasure the little gifts. You learn to have a different perspective. A more focused perspective. These smaller joys produce a spirit of gratitude. Don't worry about what you don't have. Be thankful for what you do have.

We left the apartment and moved into the newly renovated house for Lee. His bedroom was right next to mine. I awoke each morning and peeked into his room to see if he was still breathing. The first thirteen years of his life had been so very difficult. I was still living in the past and uncertain about Lee's future. I gave my worries to the Lord and then, I picked them right back up. We find joy for each day and fear sneaks back in.

I clearly remember waking up one morning and deciding I did not want to continue to live in this fear. This was another pivotal point in my life. Through prayer and God's help, I changed my attitude to one of embracing each day with joy and thankfulness. No more dreading about Lee. Letting go and letting God! Choosing contentment.

> *"I know what it is to be in need, and I know what it is to have plenty. I have learned the secret of being content in any and every situation, whether well fed or hungry, whether living in plenty or in want. I can do everything through him who gives me strength" (Philippians 4:12-13).*

I adjusted my attitude because of God's faithfulness. Lee had survived thirteen years and was happy and living as full a life as he could. As far as Lee knew, life was wonderful! I had come to this place of contentment in my life. Contentment is not found in circumstances. We still had difficult days. But contentment, just like joy and peace, is found in a Person, the Lord Jesus Christ. I continued to grow in this wisdom and understanding drawing closer to Him deepening my faith. I was going to trust God no matter the circumstances.

> *"I guide you in the way of wisdom and lead you along straight paths" (Proverbs 4:11).*

Lee had the sweetest personality, but could be a little stinker when he wanted to be. He had the most wonderfully demonstrative expressions to distinguish his likes and dislikes. And there was no mistaking the difference. If he was not happy or wanted something, he drew his eyebrows together and stuck out his tongue. If he was happy, his little cockeyed smile lit up the room. Lee's face was the focal point of his personality. Somehow I could see God's joy come through his eyes. There was a sparkle in them that was special. John and I had come to believe that Lee had an understanding far beyond his capability to communicate. He could make me laugh out loud and he enjoyed when I laughed. Bless his heart. Unfortunately for him, there was no escaping my singing. And I sang all the time.

Lee started in a program for children with disabilities when he was sixteen months old. He continued in the public school program at the McCarthy-Teszler School. He loved going to school with all the activities and his friends. He did not enjoy Christmas break because that was too long away from his regular routine and friends.

Each morning when I dropped Lee off in his classroom, I shared with them the details of his night or morning and may go into a longer conversation than necessary. Lee, graciously, gave me a few minutes to relay the information and then, by starting to fuss, he expressed to me that my time was up. It was time for me to depart and for him to get the attention of the staff. They told me as soon as I left, he was fine. I kept teasing him he was not going to hurt my feelings by giving me my marching orders. The teachers got tickled with Lee. Like I said, he could be a little stinker.

Lee went on to develop lifelong friends from school. Prom was held each year and Lee was right there dressed in a red bowtie and vest and red high-top sneakers. I called him my stud-muffin. Although, I don't think he really enjoyed the bow tie. He danced with everyone or so we were told. Parents were not invited. This was an exceptional school where all of Lee's needs were met to help him grow and be all that he could be. The support he received was imperative to his quality of life. He graduated with cap and gown at the age of 21.

He went on to The Charles Lea Center for adults with special needs. The Visions Program was created to care for people who were considered medically fragile with disabilities. This was the first program of its kind in the state. Spartanburg, South Carolina, is blessed with some of the finest programs in the Southeast. For that reason, we stayed in this caring community.

We were thankful beyond words with the many people God brought into our lives. There are not enough words to express our sincere gratitude for their help, support, skills, friendship, and prayers. From doctors to nurses to teachers to aides to therapists and many, many more that helped make Lee's life full and happy! They all helped John and me fulfill our promise to Lee after his near death experience in NICU, that we would do all we could to see that he had a happy and healthy life. His glorious smile could melt my heart. He had an iridescent glow about him. Lee had a pureness and sweetness about him that assured me of God's love.

> *"Let us draw near to God with a sincere heart in full assurance of faith . . . " (Hebrews 10:22a)*

Joni Eareckson Tada says, "To have full assurance of faith comes from trials. Faith that is full grown and come of age. Faith that gives spiritual sight into spiritual realities, helping us to be far more certain of things we do not see."[1]

At this time, Brad was on Lee's heels of becoming a teenager. He was your typical teenager, but such a sweet son, most of the time. He enjoyed picking on his mom and irritating his brother, just like all brothers do! They tell me that is how boys and men (John) show their affection. Through the years, they showed me great affection,

He swam year round, following in his dad's footsteps. John had swum for the University of South Carolina. Brad would eventually swim on an athletic scholarship at Davidson College. He enjoyed learning and therefore, excelled in school. He also loved sports, I can't begin to record all of his accomplishments in or out of the pool. He worked hard at everything he pursued. Again, as the saying goes, "the apple doesn't fall too far from the tree." Brad looked like his dad and was a high achiever like his dad.

But for me, the two things that are utmost in my heart about Brad are: first, how much he loved his brother. They had a unique, sweet relationship. The second was how he could make me laugh which is what I missed most when he went off to college. Before college, Brad came home and regaled us with funny stories from his day. I was so thankful that God had brought Brad into our lives. John and I were blessed to have raised this thoughtful, compassionate young man.

When he was in first grade he came home and told me he wanted to take Lee to school for Show and Tell. I was not quite sure about this or the reaction of his teacher. I called her and she thought it was a wonderful idea. I didn't want to have the children sit there and watch Lee in his wheelchair. I wanted them to understand that he was just like them, but, with special needs that required special equipment.

So, on the assigned day for Show and Tell, I dressed Lee up and put on his tennis shoes with white socks. We had adaptive equipment to show how people with disabilities just needed extra help. I felt it was important for them to touch Lee and see he was just a little boy who sat in a wheelchair. I took lotion and explained we rubbed his body for tactile stimulation. Each table of students took turns coming up and rubbing lotion on

Lee's arms and legs. It was an easy opportunity for them to experience Lee. The children seemed to get comfortable instantly rubbing lotion on Lee's arms and legs and he loved the attention. Their little hands were covered in clay dirt from recess. When we left, I looked down and saw red clay all over his white socks. It was from those small hands that had rubbed lotion on Lee's tiny, thin legs. I left in tears knowing that Lee had touched their lives in some special way that day. Brad took his brother to Show and Tell all through grammar school.

Years later, whenever I ran into some of Brad's old classmates, they always asked about Lee. Because of Brad's love for his brother, and taking him to Show and Tell, Lee had many friends. I don't think we'll truly understand how God used those Show and Tell opportunities, how Lee's life touched so many in ways we won't know until we get to Heaven. God had a different plan for Lee's life. He told me later that Lee had fulfilled his destiny. Oh, how we should all pray that when we stand before God in Heaven, we'd hear those words.

Brad graduated from Spartanburg High School with honors and then went off to college. That was a hard time for John, Lee, and me. There was an empty chair at dinner. But again life continues on. Lee so enjoyed when Brad came home. I also believe he loved the undivided attention he got when Brad went back to school. Lee was spoiled before Brad left. Then, he just became spoiled rotten! And he had every right to be spoiled!

"God is our refuge and strength, an ever-present help in trouble" (Psalm 46:1).

FIVE

A Holy Time

*"Do not be anxious about anything, but in everything
by prayer and petition, with thanksgiving,
present your requests to God."*
Philippians 4:6

As the years went by, John and I knew that children with the medical issues and disabilities Lee had, usually did not fare well into their twenties. Lee had far exceeded the doctor's expectations when he was born. But, there was still great uncertainty about Lee's future. So, in his early twenties, I started praying for God to prepare me for when the time came for Him to take Lee home. We had ventured down this path before and I could not fathom how I could survive letting him go. We worked diligently to meet all of Lee's needs. I did what I could do and God did the rest. We simply walked by faith. After a lifetime of trusting God, my faith continued to grow stronger and stronger.

I came to the understanding in God's eyes Lee was perfect. We looked past the physical challenges into his sweet personality, Lee had a pure heart. He was a gift from God and I would not have changed a hair on his head. We would do everything in our power with God's strength and guidance to care for Lee and provide for him a wonderful life. The challenges were great, but God always met us where we were and helped us get to the other side. Some days we went from moment to moment. Through it all I knew I needed to have a right heart and right attitude. Lee deserved to feel and know these positive feelings.

So, I prayed continuously for God to help me and then came another pivotal point in my life. As was our normal routine after school, Lee and I were in his bedroom preparing him for a nap. It was a beautiful sunny spring day. Lee had had a good day at school. It was not a difficult period in Lee's life at that time.

Which causes me to pause...the first thirteen years of Lee's life consisted of difficult days and a good day thrown in for good measure now and then. After my experience with God when I told Him I would give Lee back to Him, the next fifteen years of Lee's life, the good days became the norm and the difficult days were few and far between. But, I digress!

After school I put Lee in his bed and suctioned out his airway. Lee had chronic lung disease and we had to suction him all the time to keep those lungs clear of mucous. I want to clarify, I was wide awake and all of a sudden I had a vision! I had never had anything like it before. It was crystal clear and vivid. There was a garden filled with beautiful flowers. I remember the sight was breathtaking. I could see a good looking man, tall and straight, walking through the garden. I knew instantly it was Lee. As quickly as it came, it was gone. I knew deep in my heart God was telling me to get ready as time was nearing for Lee to go to Heaven. How tender of God to show me such an image in my vision. Lee was tall and walking. I didn't see his face, but I could tell by his gait he was happy and well. It was wonderful, but at the same time, a reminder of how fragile Lee's life was. There wasn't a sense of urgency. Lee was at a great place in his life. He was happy and healthy. We would live each day fully and thankfully. I would cherish these days.

> *"Cast your cares on the Lord and he will sustain you; he will never let the righteous fall" (Psalm 55:22).*

Three years passed since my vision from God and life was good. Then, Lee started having trouble with his lungs. His body was failing. He had grown weary. He developed a bacterial infection in his lungs the doctors could not treat. His ministry was coming to an end here on earth. God had allowed us to love Lee for 27 years. I thought no one could possibly love my boy's more than me. Then God tenderly told me my love could not compare to His love for Lee. His capacity for love was endless. It was time for Lee to go home to be with the Lord. He had fought the good fight!

A few days before Lee went to be with the Lord, God whispered in my right ear. This was the only time I have heard God audibly. It was early morning and I was coming out of sleep and He said to me just as clear as could be, "Relax and enjoy this day!" Again, I knew instantly what He was telling me. I was already grieving. I took a step back and took time to be in the moment. I smelled Lee and loved on him and drank in all I could. Through all the years of caring for Lee, God had continued to fine-tune my hearing. I had learned to listen to God and knew His voice. I was thankful for those words. God was guiding me step by step.

"He wakens me morning by morning, wakens my ear to listen like one being taught" (Isaiah 50:4b).

November 8, 2009, God sent the angels to take Lee home. He has been in Heaven over ten years now and this is still the most difficult thing for me to write about. I can't wait to see him in Heaven!

John and Brad were preparing to go to the funeral home. They did not want me to go concerned I would not be able to handle it emotionally. We got a phone call from the funeral home saying we could come. I just knew I needed to go and make sure he was okay. When I saw him, he looked like he was taking a nap, so peaceful and beautiful. I leaned over and told him that he needed to go and do all the things his little body could not do while on this earth. I wanted him to run and eat and talk and do everything his heart desired. Then, I wanted him to come back and let me know he was alright. It fills me with such joy picturing Lee with those frail legs that wouldn't hold him, kneeling with his new body before Christ! Lee was now in the Father's arms in inexpressible joy.

The day of Lee's service was one of the most holy experiences of my life. The presence of the Holy Spirit was palpable! The air around us was static, almost electric. An indescribable peace came over me. And our precious Lord orchestrated that day in perfect detail.

The service was one of celebration. All the doctors and teachers and therapists and whoever helped Lee over the years sat up front. We wanted to recognize them for their care and love for Lee through the years. I wanted a choir to sing and raise the roof off the church in celebration. But, there was not enough time to get them together. Our minister said it would have been a first for our church to have a choir singing in celebration at a funeral. We did have percussion instruments and sang wonderful hymns. Again, I believe a first for our church. Over the church was a rainbow, God giving me assurance of His nearness. In the midst of grief, as believers, we have this amazing hope. One day there will be no more tears. Tears are only temporary. But, it is difficult to let go of those we love.

One of the hymns we sang was "Sweet, Sweet Spirit." It is a song of hope and comfort. I knew the Spirit of the Lord was in that place. We were lifting our hearts in praise. It had been a cloudy, rainy day. As soon as the service started, the clouds broke and the sun came streaming in through the stained glass windows. You could feel the presence of the Lord.

> *"For the Lamb at the center of the throne will be their shepherd; he will lead them to springs of living water. And God will wipe away every tear from their eyes" (Revelation 7:17).*

It was December 1, almost a month since Lee had gone to Heaven and John and I were planning to go to the tree lighting in downtown Spartanburg. Grieving is exhausting and I had laid my head back on the couch in our den. I thought I would rest before going and closed my eyes when suddenly I heard Lee. There he was right before me, standing arms wide open and ecstatic to show me his body. I know it was his spirit, but there he was. He said with the most exuberance, "Mom, check it out!"

I told him how happy I was for him and he was gone. There was such excitement and joy in his sweet voice since Lee was nonverbal. What a thrill to hear him. God allowed him to come back and let me know he was okay. I was so thankful for this incredible gift. I stare up at the stars now and think of him and know he is beyond joyful.

Still, I grieved Lee's passing for months on end. Color seemed to fade away. There was an emptiness that remained. I was so happy for Lee being with Jesus and his new freedom. But, my heart was broken. I had cared for Lee for 27 years! I was constantly listening for him. He was always near to me. I had always taken care of him. And in the end, I couldn't make him better. How do you let go?

The only thing I knew to do was to crawl up into Jesus' lap. I believe the Lord was calling me to come to Him. So every morning I sat in the same corner of our couch with Bible in hand and some devotionals. Leaning in on my Lord and Savior brought me a comfort I couldn't find anywhere else. I drank in His Word which truly was a balm to my soul.

> *"The cords of death entangled me, the anguish of the grave came upon me; I was overcome by trouble and sorrow. Then I called on the name of the Lord: O Lord save me" (Psalm 116:3-4).*

He drew me deeper and deeper in His arms. I found He quieted my mind and calmed my soul. There was a restful peace I found leaning in on God and His Word.

> *"The Lord is my shepherd. I shall not be in want. He makes me lie down in green pastures, he leads me beside quiet waters, he restores my soul. He guides me in paths of righteousness for his name's sake. Even though I walk through the valley of the shadow of death, I will fear no evil, for you are with me, your rod and your staff they comfort me" (Psalm 23:1-4).*

I had read those same verses all my life and never did they speak to me as they did during this time. The Living Word of God speaks to us at just the right moment; exactly what we need to hear. The dark valley is a place to go through, but not a place to stay in. We must be in The Word! If we don't take advantage of this amazing gift from God, what are we missing?

Grieving is such a selfish process. I was just trying to keep my head above water and John and I grieved so differently. He knew Lee was well and went back to work where he stayed busy. That helped him to get through. It was a struggle at times. For me life seemed to stop. I could not walk into Lee's room for over a year. The grief swelled up in me and overwhelmed me. In the beginning, I tried to cry in the shower where John couldn't hear me. I knew he was so worried about me. Not long after Lee was in Heaven, I was in the shower on my knees sobbing uncontrollably. Through the tears I heard singing. It was the song "Love Lifted Me." Just the chorus,

> "Love lifted me!
> Love lifted me!
> When nothing else could help
> Love lifted me."[2]

This was a song from my childhood in church. And here I was hearing it as if someone was singing over me. I stood up and started singing at the top of my lungs. God's love lifted me up from my grief and I was singing! Only our loving God could do that. At a time when I so desperately needed comfort, God sang over me. Later I would read in Scripture:

> *"The Lord your God is with you, he is mighty to save. He will take great delight in you, he will quiet you with his love, he will rejoice over you with singing" (Zephaniah 3:17).*

> *"Record my lament; list my tears on your scroll - are they not in your record?" (Psalm 56:8).*

God knows our tears. Scripture tells us He knows the number of hairs on our heads. He wants us to have a heavenly perspective. It makes us look differently at life on earth. Earth is not our final destination. We should have an excitement and anticipation of our home in Heaven. God wants us to know the reality of Heaven's nearness. It's just past the tip of our noses!

"Lift up your eyes to the Heavens..." (Isaiah 51:6).

SIX

God's Assurance

"Praise be to the God and Father of our Lord Jesus Christ, the Father of compassion and the God of all comfort, who comforts us in all our troubles, so that we can comfort those in any trouble with the comfort we ourselves have received from God."
2 Corinthians 1:3-4

Scripture tells us we live in a fallen world. Sin came into the world in the Garden of Eden when Adam and Eve didn't believe God. This act of rebellion resulted in death coming into the world. For believers in Christ, because of His death, His burial and Resurrection, we have hope, the hope of eternity. It's the living now that can be hard. But, if we have eyes to see, God will amaze us.

> *"Therefore, just as sin entered the world through one man, and death through sin, and in this way death came to all men, because all sinned." (Romans 5:12).*

Outside our sunroom was a family of cardinals. Through the previous year, they seemed to appear just when I needed reassurance. That beautiful red bird always made me smile and gave me a lift. The cardinal became our sign of hope. Whenever we saw one, we knew God was reminding us of His presence. And He is always near.

My Bible Study ladies went up to Hendersonville, North Carolina, to have lunch. The gift shop where we were having lunch was decorated for Christmas. As we wandered around the shop, I suddenly heard the girls calling my name. Almost shouting! I went upstairs to see thousands of cardinals everywhere. They were absolutely everywhere you looked. We were totally surrounded by beautiful red cardinals. The ladies knew the cardinal was our sign of hope and they were thrilled over God's goodness.

As spring approached, Lee's birthday was nearing, along with Mother's Day and I was feeling anxious about facing those days. I had asked my dear friends to please pray for me. A mom and pop cardinal sang outside our sunroom for the three days before Lee's birthday. They sang constantly. I'm sure they had always been there. But, God had opened my eyes to His wonder.

It had been a tough eleven months. I was going through the motions, but still felt as if I was walking in a fog. Every day I sat with the Lord and I knew He had been slowly mending my heart back together. John and I were struggling to find our new rhythm. He was under a great deal of stress at the bank and also I think he missed the person he married. We actually, at one time, talked about a short separation. I believe grieving over a child is the hardest thing a couple can go through. We never followed through on the separation. We had always been a team through thick and thin, but, I never thought we would actually say the words. We made a covenant before God and earnestly loved one another. God would hold us together and see us through.

I knew Lee was well. God had given me assurance of that. I was thrilled for Lee and his being in the presence of our Lord. He was finally free from the confined body he had on this earth. But, I was still struggling. I heard someone teaching and they said sometimes our prayers need to be very specific. As simple as that, be specific. I was tired of being tired and tired of being sad. I missed me. I knew John was missing me. I, also, knew for me to do whatever God had planned for me, I needed to find my joy. I needed for the 'old' Lynne to return.

So, I prayed that morning for God to help me find my joy. I prayed specifically for the Lord to help me find myself; my energy; my enthusiasm. When I finished my devotion the cloud had lifted. I don't know if I had reached that point in my grief where I was able to move forward or if God was ready for me to move forward or I was at a place where I could give myself permission to be happy. I think God was orchestrating all three. Lee loved it when I was happy and laughed when I laughed. I knew he wanted me to be happy and was cheering me on in Heaven. I read somewhere that when the time is right, God will prompt you to ask for healing of some brokenness in your life. There is no substitute for God's direction.

For years, I had lived with the reality of Heaven. Lee was very sick the first half of his life and we never knew how long God would let us keep him. Both my parents had died before Lee. But, not until Lee was in Heaven did the reality of it open wide in my heart and mind.

Open my eyes that I may see
Glimpses of truth Thou hast for me; ...
Open my eyes, illumine me, Spirit divine!
Clara H. Scott[3]

"He will wipe every tear from their eyes. There will be no more death or mourning or crying or pain, for the old order of things has passed away" (Revelation 21:4).

"However, as it is written: "No eye has seen, nor ear has heard, no mind has conceived what God has prepared for those who love him." (1 Corinthians 2:9)

In October of 2010, coming up on Lee's first year in Heaven, John and I decided to go to the beach and celebrate Lee being with Jesus. As I look back, I believe God was giving us just a hint of Heaven! It was God's special gift for John and me.

We arrived at our favorite place, a little condo at a point on Fripp Island, South Carolina. From our position, you could see the ocean on two sides. It had always been a place of rest for me. Nothing special with two bedrooms and a glider positioned right in front of the sliding glass door looking out at the ocean. I could sit in that glider and gaze at the ocean all day. There was a peace about this place.

On this trip the ocean was as calm as a lake, even when the tide came in. There was a rock wall between the building and the ocean. We had been there before when the water was washing over the rock wall. But, on this occasion, it was amazingly calm.

Dolphins were eating near the sea-wall. They were close enough you could hear them blow air out of the air-holes. They gently glided through the water in pairs. We had never seen them closer.

That night there was a full moon shining down on the water. John was walking by the glass doors and saw what looked like sparklers under the water. The light was jumping around in the water like little fireflies. It was the most mesmerizing thing to watch. As quickly as it came, it was gone. It seemed to be the angle of the full moon on the small ripples of water over this calm sea.

The next day, the air was full of dragon flies and butterflies. They were absolutely everywhere, hundreds of them. It was like we had walked into a dream. The dragonflies darted everywhere and had wingspans over four inches wide. The butterflies were yellow, orange monarchs, pairs of small deep orange butterflies. It was fascinating to take all this in. We were in sensory overload.

The following day was beautiful. The sun was bright and the waves were crashing on the sea-wall with a cool breeze. The dolphins were putting on a show for us. They swam past our condo and did incredible flips in the air. They were more active than usual. Our guess was that they were probably mating or battling for territory. None the less, it was fun to watch!

The full moon was later rising this evening and was a wonderful orange/pink. They called it a "Harvest Moon" on television. It was huge and shining down over the ocean. I couldn't get enough of seeing it and its spectacular color. It was so big and beautiful. I loved watching how its light danced on the waves.

We were leaving on Sunday and I couldn't sleep. It had been an unbelievable time! I got up early to wait for the sunrise. I listened as the waves crashed on the rocks at high tide. Then I saw a shooting star and it felt like Lee kissed me on the cheek. In the dark, still night with just the stars and the beautiful water, it felt like he reached down from Heaven and touched my right cheek. It was one of those moments that literally took my breath away.

We have an awesome God! I'm still in awe of our loving Father. John and I had gone to celebrate Lee in Heaven. But God had another plan instead. He overwhelmed us with gifts from Heaven. If we could but peek behind the veil of Heaven to see what God has instore for us.

> *"So we fix our eyes not on what is seen, but on what is unseen. For what is seen is temporary, but what is unseen is eternal" (2 Corinthians 4:18).*

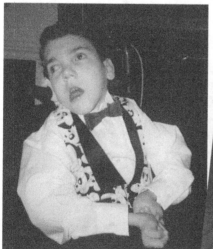

17. Lee on prom night with his red bow-tie.

18. Brad and Lee on Easter Sunday 1999.

19. John and Brad at high school swim meet 2001.

20. John, me, Brad and Lee at Lee's graduating ceremony from The McCarthy-Teszler School.

21. Lee looking happy and healthy 2005.

22. Family picture before Brad left for college courtesy of Terrill Photography, Spartanburg, South Carolina.

23. Me and Brad at Davidson College, Davidson, North Carolina.

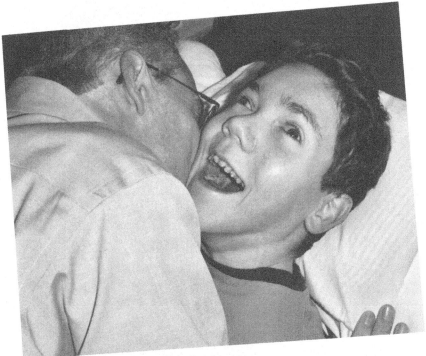

24. Lee loved when his dad played with him.

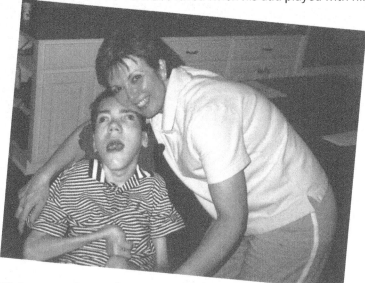

25. Lee was, almost always, at my side.

26. Brad home from college. Lee's face would light up as soon as he heard Brad's voice.

27. Brad competing for Davidson College in swimming.

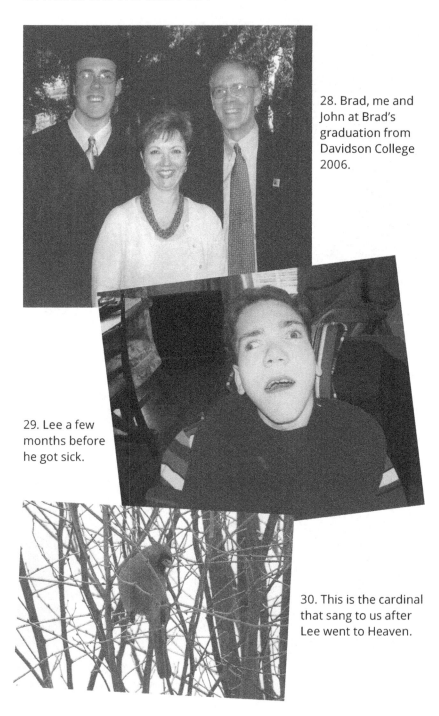

28. Brad, me and John at Brad's graduation from Davidson College 2006.

29. Lee a few months before he got sick.

30. This is the cardinal that sang to us after Lee went to Heaven.

SEVEN

Rejoice In the Small Things

"My grace is sufficient for you for my power
is made perfect in weakness."
2 Corinthians 12:9a

December of 2010 I was preparing a lesson for my circle at church for our Christmas gathering. I had seen written in some magazine a sweet story called "Keep Your Fork." As it goes, there are special occasion dinners at Grandma's house, which were much anticipated events. There were lots of cousins, aunts, uncles, sometimes a neighbor or two; all talking at once and jostling for a position at the tables. As aunts and older cousins cleared away the main course, we were often told, "Keep your fork." Music to our ears! Those words always meant that something better was just about to be set in front of us, if we could be patient for a moment. Maybe scrumptious banana pudding, pound cake, pecan pie, pumpkin pie ….

Something truly extraordinary and wonderful, something to look forward to was on the way.

Everyone needs a gentle reminder that, "the best is yet to come!"

I know that Heaven awaits us and when we go through difficult times our hope in Christ is that the best is yet to come! I made copies of the story; bought forks and tied red ribbons on them to give to the ladies. But, as I was preparing my devotion, I kept being drawn to Scripture saying "Don't be afraid!" Every Scripture had the same message. The words seemed to jump off the page. God seemed to be pointing them out to me over and over again. I thought there must be someone in the group that really needed to hear this message. "Don't be afraid!" It didn't dawn on me until a few years later when I stumbled upon this devotion and realized it had been me. God was preparing me for the journey that lay before us.

On February 7, 2011, I went in for my annual mammogram. What was to be a routine test turned into a journey that would require faith and endurance for John and me. I would go on to have biopsies on both breasts and discover I had stage one cancer in the left breast. When the radiologists sat us down to give us the news it was as if the world stopped for a moment. You always dread the "C" word. But, there is no way to prepare for it. I leaned into John and cried. John said it was like the wind had been knocked out of his lungs. I think it was the shock of it all. We had been through so much over the past year. But, God had sustained us. I had experienced God's hand in incredible ways. And once you've experienced God, really come into His presence, you're never quite the same. There is a peace and a trust, knowing that God is in full control. You just have to let go and let God! As crazy as it sounds, I came to a place of total peace. I didn't worry and I didn't cry again. The peace of God that transcends our understanding does not make sense. But, I can tell you it is a reality. The Holy Spirit will provide for all your needs.

> *"Be joyful in hope, patient in affliction, faithful in prayer"*
> *(Romans 12:12).*

I had taken female hormones for over twenty years. And I would do it again. I struggled for several years with extreme mood swings and anxiety or severe premenstrual syndrome. A wonderful gynecologist worked with me for a year to get my hormones where they needed to be. John and

I have always agreed that quality of life is far better than quantity of life. I can assure you that with hormone treatment, quality of life was much better for all within my sphere. We, also, knew that by taking hormones, there was an increase chance of breast cancer. So with this cancer diagnosis, the first task was to get off hormones. So I stopped cold turkey. It's like going through menopause instantly. It was definitely a challenging couple of weeks to say the least. And all before I had surgery or started treatment.

This would be the beginning of a long, difficult test of endurance! I had surgery in March to remove lymph nodes to see if the cancer had spread and a lumpectomy to remove the cancer from the breast. The blessing was the cancer had not spread to the lymph nodes. The difficult part was the cancer cells were aggressive, which for those who know me that was probably not a surprise. I tend to work hard at everything I do. I had a port placed in my shoulder where the needle went for the infusions. I started treatment every 21 days for a total of four treatments.

> *"And we know that in all things God works for the good of those who love him, who have been called according to his purpose" (Romans 8:28).*

I have to sincerely say at this point, I was not angry about the situation we found ourselves in. I never once worried about the outcome. I had learned to walk from faith to faith. We were going to take this one step at a time and trust God for the rest!

Jesus Calling for March 11 says "When I gave you My Spirit, I empowered you to live beyond your natural ability and strength . . . The issue is not your strength but Mine, which is limitless. By walking close to me, you can accomplish My purposes in My strength." [4]

> *"I sought the Lord, and he answered me;*
> *He delivered me from all my fears.*
> *Those who look to him are radiant;*
> *Their faces are never covered with shame.*

This poor man called, and the Lord heard him;
He saved him out of all his troubles.
The angel of the Lord encamps around those who fear
Him, and he delivers them.
Taste and see that the Lord is good;
Blessed is the man who takes refuge in him." (Psalm 34:4-8)

During this time I held fast to these words. There would be days I held on with both hands, honestly, with everything I had. After I didn't have the energy to hold on, I knew God was holding on to me. Again, Jesus was my refuge. As Scripture tells us, He is an ever present help in times of trouble.

Again, I was learning to rejoice in the small things. You start to see that our Lord is in the smallest of details. This was a lesson we had learned through Lee. After an infusion, three weeks were just hanging on. Then in the fourth week, I started to rise back up and have some energy. There would be days when walking a few houses down the street and back was a big accomplishment. Thankfully, spring had arrived and I would have beautiful days to get outside. My hair started to come out and we had a shaving party with my neighbors across the street, because Jim had clippers and we didn't. I told Jim that when he first moved in, I'm sure that he never thought he would help shave a ladies head. I was never sad about my hair. I never wore a wig. It was spring into summer and much too hot for a wig. I had dear friends bring me hats and one that had a pony tail hanging out the back! I took the opportunity to buy a few myself. I had always loved hats. I had dyed my hair for too many years to count. Now, we would see just how white my hair truly was.

The chemotherapy was a physical challenge for me. Not all experience the same side effects. I had debilitating fatigue. There were days I couldn't lift my head off the pillow. My care was wonderful though. I only remember getting sick one time during the four treatments. I also had three medications to help keep me from getting sick. The chemotherapy caused my white blood count to drop which resulted in my immune system being compromised. I was put in isolation to allow the count to come back up. After each of the four treatments I was put into isolation. The longest would be sixteen days. The shot they gave me to build my white blood cells caused my bones to hurt all over. With much difficulty, I got into a hot bath, usually around midnight and soaked. Amazing what a hot bath can do. I visited the emergency room only one time because of chest pain. Turned out, I had decided not to take an over-the-counter medication that helped ease the pain from the shot, which helped my white blood cells. I never missed that medication again.

Brad was working in New Hampshire during this time and flew home to see me. I can't begin to tell you how that boosted my spirits. He and John shaved their heads to support me. Brad was constantly checking on me. And my sweet husband had to walk far outside his comfort zone to care for me. He was always leaving notes before work giving me encouragement for the day. Bless his heart! We were traveling another very difficult road together.

I've heard it said you get to know God when there is nothing left. Emotionally I had nothing left and physically I was on my knees. There were days when I didn't have the strength to pray. The peace of God comes from knowing God is in control. I was clinging to His promises. I knew He would see me through.

> *"In the same way, the Spirit helps us in our weakness. We do not know what we ought to pray for, but the Spirit himself intercedes for us with groans that words cannot express"* (Romans 8:26).

I was so grateful during this time. Many, many wonderful people prayed for me and I could feel their prayers. Members of our church came (including my minister and his wife) wearing hats and sang hymns with me. I cherish those memories. They uplifted my soul. My sister, Cindy, was in constant communication. She is a nurse and unfortunately, had gone through cancer herself. All these people God had placed in my life, I called my pearls on my string of life. I had heard a speaker say this at a presentation and I just loved the image.

On a side note, at that same presentation I wore a pretty white hat and as with chemo, when you lose your hair, you lose all your hair. No eyelashes, no eyebrows, no shaving my legs. Yay! So, I had put on false eyelashes for this luncheon. The speaker said things that touched my heart and I started to tear up. I suddenly realized my beautiful eyelashes were coming off. The sweet lady next to me saw what was happening and we just started laughing uncontrollably. Here I was with lashes in hand and a bald head to match and it was hysterical. Sometimes you just have to laugh. It is truly good for the soul.

I survived after enduring the four chemotherapy treatments. Although there were days I was not sure that would be the case. Praise God. I was able to ring that bell declaring I was finished with my chemotherapy treatments. I had written in my journal that after I finished my treatments I lay in the bed experiencing an amazing rest like no other. My body was actually enjoying the pleasure of rest, which it so needed. The ravages of the chemo had subsided and the aching effects of the shot had dissipated and I was just lying there. I could actually feel the sheets and my body was finally in this calm rest. This extraordinary rest was an unbelievable experience that I can only compare to being in that calm, restful peace with the Lord.

I finished the chemotherapy at the end of May. This was the first half of the journey. I would begin radiation the first of July. I would have radiation five days a week for six weeks. But, for the time being, I was enjoying feeling better. I could drink my coffee, which I couldn't during treatment. Tasted like metal. My hair started growing back as white as snow. But, we were moving forward with God's amazing grace!

> *"But those who hope in the Lord will renew their strength. They will soar on wings like eagles; they will run and not grow weary, they will walk and not be faint" (Isaiah 40:31).*

EIGHT

A Fountain of Joy

Enter his gates with thanksgiving and his courts with praise;
Give thanks to him and praise his name.
For the Lord is good and his love endures forever;
His faithfulness continues through all generations.
Psalm 100:4-5

As we continued on this arduous journey, I started my radiation treatment. The side effect for me with radiation was fatigue, which is a common side effect. Fifteen days in and it hit me. I still hadn't recovered from the chemo-therapy treatment. My oncologist heard about a Mayo Clinic Study which suggested taking ginseng. So, I promptly ordered it from the pharmacy which used organic ginseng. I'm convinced it helped me get through the rest of the radiation without napping all day. A nap and not pushing it and I made it to the thirtieth day!

I can't begin to tell you how thrilled I was to come to the end of this road. I honestly don't want to travel that road again. But, God so gently carried me through this storm and He lovingly delivered me to the end. There was a fountain outside of our cancer center. I walked past that fountain every day that I went for chemo-therapy and radiation. It was hot and humid when I finished on August 18. The sound of the water drew my attention, especially when I was feeling the fatigue. And the heat and humidity made it difficult to breath. So on my last day of radiation, after I rang that sweet bell, I jumped into that fountain. I was finally going to enjoy those cool waters that had called me and celebrate the end of a long and stormy road and take the plunge. What a celebration surrounded by family, friends, doctors, nurses and many more.

As I walked that path over seven months, a scripture I held fast to was:

> *"Be joyful always; pray continually; give thanks in all circumstances, for this is God's will for you in Christ Jesus" (1Thessalonians 5:16-18).*

God is not asking us to give thanks for the tough roads, but that we give thanks in them. I've learned to be thankful in all circumstances. This is not a feeling but a choice. We have an awesome God who will move heaven and earth to fulfill His purpose in our lives. God's peace had been profound for me over those past two years.

If we are paying attention, God has a way of confirming things. In my devotion, *Diamond's In The Dust*, by Joni Eareckson Tada, August 23, on which I read five days after I jumped into the fountain.[5]

> *"On that day a fountain will be opened to the house of David the inhabitants of Jerusalem, to cleanse them from sin and impurity" (Zechariah 13:1).*

"A fountain is a place of joy. God has opened up a fountain to you through the Lord Jesus. He invites you to come on in and enjoy His love. Don't stand on the edges of his joy. He has washed away your sin and you, like a child, can be free and full of life."

I proclaim a fountain is a place of joy. That day it was my celebration of completing this journey, filled with joy, knowing Jesus was right beside me and at times carried me. It would take another six months to start to feel like myself again. But, as I write this, I am almost ten years cancer free!

> *"For with you is the fountain of life; in your light we see light." (Psalm 36:9)*

I heard God calling me after my treatments. I was jumping in the fountain to refresh me, quenching my spiritual thirst after being in the desert for so long. It was glorious.

My faithful Bible Study friends gave me a celebration party at the end of that arduous journey. You are so thankful to have crossed the finish line, I wrote the following to share:

I'm so thankful for God's strength, hope, joy, His glorious presence and constant encouragement.

I'm thankful for John stepping out of his comfort zone to care for me, even when things were really difficult.

I'm thankful for my hair growing back, including my eyebrows and eyelashes.

I'm thankful that Brad called his mama every day to check in on me and flew home often from New Hampshire.

I'm thankful that my boys loved me so much that they shaved their heads too.

I'm thankful that my hands are much better and I can put on some of my shoes.

I'm thankful for the internet to be able to hear from all of my precious pearls during this long journey.

I'm thankful to be able to wear a bra again. I can now take off the sweaters I wore all summer.

I'm thankful I'm starting to feel like myself again.

I'm thankful for all the doctors and staff that took great care of me.

I'm thankful for the lake house God placed before us for me to find rest and His amazing peace.

I'm thankful that I've learned to swim and so enjoy it.

I'm thankful for all the pearls on my necklace of life. For all the special people God has brought into my path to give me strength and encouragement along the way, especially your prayers.

I'm thankful for my sister, Cindy, who called every day to give me encouragement and wonderful advice since she had been through cancer herself.

I'm thankful that God continues to bless me with His assurance that Lee is wonderful in Heaven.

Even in the most difficult times there is always something to be thankful for. God will give you a Heavenly perspective and that changes everything. Evidences of God's grace and goodness are everywhere. Even in the darkest of places, His light will shine the brightest.

> *"May the God of hope fill you with all joy and peace as you trust in Him, so that you may overflow with hope by the power of the Holy Spirit" (Romans 15:13).*

31. Me and John after starting my chemotherapy 2011.

32. John, me and Brad after my last chemotherapy treatment. Brad surprised me by flying home and organizing a celebration with friends.

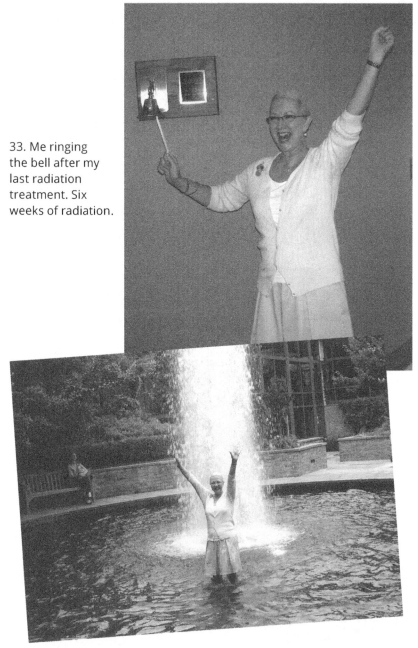

33. Me ringing the bell after my last radiation treatment. Six weeks of radiation.

34. Me in my fountain of joy. I could not have been more excited to have made it to the end of this long journey.

NINE

Angels from Heaven

*"For he will command his angels concerning you
to guard you in all your ways."*
Psalm 91:11

In January of 2013, I went in for my mammogram. They found calcification in my breast and wanted to do a biopsy. Needless to say this news sent shock waves through me. I was not expecting the news about a biopsy. I was taking aspirin so we had to wait a week for the procedure. For those who have been in this situation, it is a terrible place to be. The uncertainty and having walked the long road such a short time ago was extremely difficult.

I had sent out a prayer request to my prayer warriors. I prayed continuously. I read Scripture. And I climbed back up into Jesus' lap. I knew He was my refuge and strength. I was holding fast to Him and His Word! I felt God had great things for me to do! I had much to share about our awesome God! I had much to learn in His Word!

Wednesday morning of that week I woke up with a new freshness and renewed hope! I had learned through Lee and his life to live each day with joy and peace. I was not going to worry or be afraid. There was an excitement for the day and a calm in my spirit. Scripture tells us

Jesus spoke and calmed the sea. How much more will He do for those who love Him?

John and I had decided to bundle all of our services with our cable company. The man from the cable company came Thursday morning and arrived exactly at 8:00 a.m. I was surprised when the doorbell rang at the designated time. As soon as I opened my front door I was greeted with this tremendous smile and this man that seemed to glow. At first, I was taken aback. I had the sense he was filled with the Holy Spirit.

"I love starting my day with such a nice smile!"

He started telling me how he was filled with joy and he lived each day with peace and to be thankful each day, which was almost verbatim my prayer that morning and I told him so.

Joyce, my Bible teacher and friend called to tell me about a meeting. I shared with her about this man and our conversation and I felt it was a confirmation from God. She told me God sends angels to bring us confirmation.

After he connected the cable, he came up from under the house praising Jesus because he had found the right cable the first time. I sat over my devotion enjoying watching him praise God. He seemed overwhelmed with God's goodness. He kept talking about how awesome God was. I love when people are not inhibited about their love for Jesus.

Somehow in the conversation I told him I had had cancer and was waiting to have another biopsy the next day. I shared with him what Joyce had said to me how God brings angels into our lives. Before I could say anything, he looked me straight in the eyes and said, "God brings you confirmation!" He took my breath away. You could feel God's presence right there. It was absolutely amazing.

He went outside to his truck. Coming back in he said, "God has placed something on my heart and can I share it with you?"

"Of, course.:

"Do you know the Bible story of the woman and the blood? She touched the hem of Jesus' garment."

I knew the story from the Bible, but I had just heard it that very morning on television!

"Yes, I know that story well."

"God told me you are healed and there is no more cancer!"

> *"Just then a woman who had been subject to bleeding for twelve years came up behind him and touched the edge of his cloak. She said to herself, "If I only touch his cloak, I will be healed." Jesus turned and saw her, "Take heart, daughter," He said, "your faith has healed you." And the woman was healed from that moment"* (Matthew 9:20-22).

All I could do was cry because I felt his words all over my body. It was the same as the day of Lee's funeral. It was as if static was all around. Then he prayed over me, blessing me and my family.

"God said He has a great plan for your life."

Wow!

To think of my angel from God that day is still astonishing. This was an unbelievable experience, but, the timing was perfect. I knew with every fiber of my being he was an angel from God. Blessed does not adequately describe that moment in my life. Another pivotal moment for me!

> *"'For I know the plans I have for you,'" declares the Lord, "plans to prosper you and not to harm you, plans to give you hope and a future'"* (Jeremiah 29:11).

The day was not over! I went to the grocery store across the street from our house. As I came into the store there were two ladies standing at the end of the frozen food section.

"You have such beautiful hair," they said.

"Thank you. It was a gift from God. I have been through cancer treatment."

They looked at me and said, "You are now cancer free."

My knees almost buckled. I thanked them again, but felt like I was in a haze. Things were happening in a supernatural way and it was almost too much for me to comprehend.

I walked farther down this aisle when two men approached me.

"May we hug you?"

Now, I was beginning to wonder if this was something like Candid Camera? I could see the store manager at the checkout down the aisle. I thought if I needed him, he was where he could hear me. I don't know why, but I told one of the gentlemen he could hug me.

He put his arms around my shoulders, but never touched me. He looked me straight in the eyes and said, "You are cancer free."

The two gentlemen walked off. I stood there for a moment trying to process what had just occurred. I ran to the car and called John and told him that he was not going to believe what had just happened in the grocery store.

I read in my devotion that very week that God allows things to prove His power! The manifestation of God in our lives helps us to see His power; His love; and His grace. These events in my life were evidences of God's grace and goodness. I would go on to have that biopsy that Friday. I told the radiologist performing the biopsy I was not worried because God had sent an angel to tell me that all was well!

"For I am the Lord, your God, who takes hold of your right hand and says to you, 'Do not fear; I will help you'" (Isaiah 41:13).

TEN

Listening To God

*"Not only so, but we also rejoice in our sufferings,
because we know that suffering produces perseverance;
perseverance, character; and character, hope."*
Romans 5:3-4

It was 2014 and for the past two years I had been studying my Bible daily, going deeper and deeper in God's Word. I found an amazing teacher, Les Feldick on television. He is an expository teacher. Les teaches by comparing Scripture with Scripture. Through Les' teachings, the Holy Spirit opened up His Word to me like never before. I was hungry for the Word and immersed myself every day in the Bible. God continued to fill me up and I have continued to study under Les for eight years. The wonderful thing is John is studying under Les also. We won't miss a day. My Bible is worn through and through and I've only touched the surface of all God would have us to know.

John was a believer when we married. But, I wanted him to know Christ on a much deeper level. I had prayed for God to draw John nearer for too many years to count. Remember as the old saying goes, be careful what you ask for! Well, God would answer my prayer. But, not the way I had expected...

John had been very involved in our church for over twenty years. He had been on Session and on too numerous committees to remember. Church was important to him, but it was more about doing, than knowing. I had grown immeasurably in my faith and my relationship with our Lord, Jesus Christ. I wanted him to have that same kind of relationship. He had witnessed the unbelievable things God had done for me during our difficult journey. I prayed for him to know Christ in the most intimate way. But I also knew that the Holy Spirit would be the One to open his eyes to the wonder of Christ and His Word.

In October of 2014, John started having memory loss and balance issues. We were walking through the grocery store and he started shuffling his feet as he walked. I knew something was terribly wrong. I called a friend who was a physician and he said John needed to see a neurologist quickly and he would help us get in to see one. They did MRI's and determined John had developed hydrocephalus, fluid on the brain. Honestly, this was a relief because they were throwing out other diagnoses with dire outcomes. The neurologist said he wanted to do a spinal tap to see if he could release the pressure. If symptoms persisted, we were to come back in four weeks. In a matter of days John was losing ground rapidly. He was having great difficulty walking and talking. He could not process simple tasks. I called the neurologist office to get the appointment for the spinal tap and could not get them to call me back. I called our friend, the physician, and he couldn't get the doctor to call him back either. I finally went and sat in the doctor's office to get the appointment and still could not see him. I could not believe I was not able to see or talk with this neurologist. As we looked back, we could see how God slammed that door shut.

Our son, Brad, works in the medical field and was trying to find a doctor in Charlotte. Our friend was working to get John into Duke University Hospital to see a doctor. It is very difficult to get into Duke quickly. By this point, John could barely stand and could not walk. His memory was going every day. We were losing ground rapidly.

By God's grace, we had an appointment with the neurosurgeon at Duke five days later. John, Brad, and I arrived at Duke anxious to meet with the doctor and get the help John needed. During our discussion, the neurosurgeon at Duke felt a spinal tap could have caused death. I sat there stunned to think how close we came to that reality. God's hand moving is a powerful thing to witness.

Before the surgery, I had called a special phone number to get a hotel room for those going to Duke for medical treatment. The lady on the line could not have been nicer. But, we needed a room in short order and they were booked. I told her the urgency for the room that my husband was coming for brain surgery. She told me to call back in the afternoon and she would check again. So, I did as requested and she was so apologetic that they still did not have an available room. Then, all of a sudden she was excited and said she couldn't believe it but a room had just opened up. I told her I wasn't surprised. God had been guiding this process. As we sat in that hotel room waiting for surgery, a cardinal kept coming up to our window. Just a reminder, He was right with us. How great is our God. It is breathtaking to see the awe and wonder of our faithful God.

John had surgery on November 10 to relieve the pressure on his brain. When he came out of recovery, they walked him down the hall and I was watching his gait. As soon as he started walking, I knew he was going to be fine. His gait was normal again. Praise God! The neurosurgeon felt John had had normal hydrocephalous since he was a young boy. He had meningitis at the age of nine which could have resulted in the hydrocephalus. When I met John, he had headaches all the time. He assumed it was sinus headaches and took medicine for sinus problems. Looking back, we now know it was the pressure on his brain. John had the flu the March before the episode. The neuro-surgeon felt that was probably what triggered the fluid buildup on the brain. It would take a year for his brain to reorient. John eventually got back to working his long hours at the bank. I told him, God was trying to get his attention. The thing about his symptoms and his brain surgery, he didn't remember much about the whole situation.

I knew God was trustworthy and kept praying God would open his heart. I had been to the Ladies Community Bible Study at our church

Wednesday morning. It was January 28, 2016. The study had been on spiritual warfare.

"Put on the full armor of God so that you can take your stand against the devil's schemes. For our struggle is not against flesh and blood, but against the rulers, against the authorities, against the powers of this dark world and against the spiritual forces of evil in the heavenly realms" (Ephesians 6:11-12).

John came home the evening of the Community Bible Study saying he had had heartburn since 3:30 that afternoon. He seemed fine and ate dinner. So we went to bed with no concerns. I must interject that John is 6 foot and weighs about 160 pounds. He has always taken care of himself and has his annual physical. He woke me up around 10:30 with his hat and coat on saying we needed to go to the hospital. I got dressed and walked into the kitchen to a counter filled with all kinds of medicine for indigestion. He was sitting on the stairs in the den. I was still trying to clear my head because he had awaken me from a sound asleep. I asked if we should call 911? I believe at this point he was frightened and said he felt we could get there faster.

As we pulled out of our garage, I could hear his breathing and realized he was in trouble. I turned on my flashers and turned onto the main road which went straight to the hospital. I was trying to remain calm and not wreck the car. It's only about five miles to the hospital. There was no traffic on the roads at that time of the night. I stopped at the red lights and if no traffic was coming, proceeded on through. I even came to a major intersection and when the cars saw my flashing lights, they let me through.

At this point, a policeman pulled in behind me. I was relieved thinking he was going to escort us to the hospital when he turned on his siren and was trying to get me to pull over. I was two blocks from the hospital and John was getting worse. We arrived at the emergency entrance and as I was getting out of the car to help John, I was surrounded by two police cars and four policemen. Poor John got out of the car and walked himself into the emergency entrance. There I was with a policeman threatening to put me in the back of his car and throw me in jail for not stopping for a blue light and for reckless driving.

He asked for my license and registration and walked back to his car. I heard within my spirit very clearly "Be still!" Only God kept me quiet that night. This policeman was keeping me from my husband and whatever was going on in that emergency room! He came back and said the car was registered to me and I had no history of tickets. Now, remember, I am a white haired, over 60 woman; driving a gray SUV. No ticket. And no apology.

John was having a heart attack. He had two stents placed in his heart and no heart damage. A miracle since he had not been feeling well since early that afternoon. Praise God again! I have to be honest. I did not handle this well. I told John that God was still trying to get his attention and he needed to start paying attention. I was still trying to be in control. I had to let go and let God.

This medical emergency finally got John's attention. The heart attack he remembered. He retired after 43 years in banking in June of 2019. The joy I have watching him grow in his faith and hunger for the Word just fills my heart to full. I needed to trust God's perfect plan and in His perfect timing. Continuing to lift prayers to the Father, I learned to be patient when God required me to wait and expect Him to fulfill the promises. He is trustworthy. The secret to peace is discovering, accepting and appreciating God's perfect timing.

> *"Consider it pure joy, my brothers, whenever you face trials of many kinds, because you know that the testing of your faith develops perseverance. Perseverance must finish its work, so that you may be mature and complete, not lacking anything" (James 1:2-4).*

Brad promised Lee to watch over us. I don't believe he knew exactly what that would entail. During all of these travails, John and I were blessed with a special daughter-in-law and a most joyful granddaughter. We enjoy spending time with Brad and his family and watching our granddaughter grow. We have come to this season of life where we are thankful for each day. Jesus has opened our eyes to live by faith and not by sight. What a remarkable way to live each day.

"We live by faith, not by sight" (2 Corinthians 5:7).

ELEVEN

God's Timing Is Perfect

"But as for me, I watch in hope for the Lord,
I wait for God my Savior;
my God will hear me."
Micah 7:7

In the book, *101 Amazing Things About Heaven*, Robin Schmidt says, "The size of our need for God never changes, only our awareness of how deeply it truly is. The magnitude of God never varies, only our perception of His greatness!"[6]

I discovered those words are so true; to come to a profound understanding of how much we need Jesus. He wants us to have a loving, intimate relationship with Him. As He draws us nearer, our perception is enlarged and our affection grows. Psalm 34:8 invites us to "taste and see that the Lord is good."

Jesus invites us to feed on His Word, to immerse ourselves in the Scripture. That is how we come to know Him in that deep, personal way. As I got lost in His Word, the Holy Spirit quickened my heart to understand. Sometimes it appeared as if the words jumped off the page.

As I sit here, it is hard to put into words what I have experienced through the years in the presence of God. Waiting in His Presence and watching to see what He would do. It has taken years for me to gain perspective on all that God has done in my life. For God to be magnified in my mind and spirit is breathtaking! There comes clarity of who God is and the awareness of the enormity of His power. I have touched God's Holiness and it was unbelievably humbling. I cannot imagine what Heaven will be like when I come into His presence.

I have come to know Jesus, really know Him in spectacular ways. During my darkest days, His love and tenderness quieted my mind, calmed my soul and ever so carefully and sweetly, day by day, mended my broken heart after Lee went to Heaven. His love is transformative and His peace profound. I have heard our Lord Jesus Christ through the Holy Spirit speak words to me. He has sent angels to reassure me.

God quickened my heart to the Scripture, His Living Word. God breathed, undeniable, sufficient Truth. I have come to that thin place where I felt the Presence of God and heard Him in His quiet whispers. God has blessed me with eyes that see, eyes of faith. When we experience God or witness the Lord's glory we can't help but be changed. To experience what God does with our obedience, with our belief, is an awesome thing.

I have been watching for almost 60 years and have been overwhelmed at what Jesus has done in and through my life. Not a path I would have chosen, but one I would not change. To have my eyes opened in wonder of God's majesty. To magnify Him in my mind and spirit is but a taste of what Heaven will be like. Seeing God's hand in the big things of life and in the smallest of details is to know God is trustworthy. When you are filled with the Holy Spirit, it enables you to be filled to full with peace that passes all understanding. Faith that helps you see with the eyes of your heart through death to eternity. This is our hope as believers. Faith robs death of its sting. Scripture mainly presents us with a view of life from the eternal perspective.

"There is a time for everything,
and a season for every activity under heaven.

> *a time to be born and a time to die,*
> *a time to plant and a time to uproot,*
> *a time to kill and a time to heal*
> *a time to tear down and a time to build,*
> *a time to weep and a time to laugh,*
> *a time to mourn and a time to dance,*
> *a time to scatter stones and a time to gather them,*
> *a time to embrace and a time to refrain,*
> *a time to search and a time to give up,*
> *a time to keep and a time to throw away,*
> *a time to tear and a time to mend,*
> *a time to be silent and a time to speak,*
> *a time for love and a time to hate,*
> *a time for war and a time for peace."*

(Ecclesiastes 3:1-8)

These Scriptures confirm that God's timing is perfect! Verse 11 of Ecclesiastes chapter three says, "God has made everything beautiful in its time." I have gone from weeping to laughing. I didn't think that was possible, but it came to pass. I have gone from mourning to dancing and remember the exact place and time when God lifted me out of the pit of despair. God has a plan if we would just be still and listen. However, in order to hear Him, we first have to know Him.

I still have on my refrigerator, placed there a few days after Lee's birth, that faded yellow note paper with the ink so faint: **Don't give up! Miracles do happen**! It's still there almost forty years later. It's hard to believe it has been a lifetime ago. A month after Lee was taken to Heaven I read in *Jesus Calling*, December 21:

"As you persevere along the path I have prepared for you, depending on My strength to sustain you,

expect to see miracles and you will.

Miracles are not always visible to the naked eye but those who live by faith can see them clearly. Living by faith rather than sight,

enables you to see My Glory."[7]

To have eyes of faith was to come to the knowledge that the miracle I had prayed for when Lee was born was not the miracle God had intended. His life was the miracle. Each and every day was a miracle!

In Philippians 4:11 Paul tells us he had learned to be content whatever the circumstances. It has not always been easy. There are still days when I get anxious and have to crawl back up into Jesus' lap. In His presence is where I find peace and safety. Through the years and the struggles, I've seen that the Lord is good. I've learned to trust Him with all my heart. He is where I take refuge. When you trust the Lord, no matter how difficult the circumstances, He has promised the journey will take you directly to the destination He has planned. That is a comfort trusting that God is still in control. There is no substitute for God's direction. Through trusting God, I have learned to be content whether in need or want.

"Wait for the Lord; be strong and take heart and wait for the Lord" (Psalm 27:14).

God uses waiting to restore our strength, renew, and teach us. It is using these waiting times by discovering what God may be trying to teach us in them. During the darkest time I grew closer, pressing in to God and growing in Christ. And when we wait, He will make our next steps clear. This has been my journey, waiting, hopefully, in God's presence and watching to see what He will do. Learning to be content in the waiting. I am a doer and not very good at waiting. But, I have learned it is a far better thing to wait on the Lord.

To delight in the Lord means to experience great joy in His presence. The definition of delight is a high degree of gratification; extreme satisfaction. That is what I feel when I pray and when I'm in His Word and sense His presence. Joy inexpressible! First Thessalonians 5:16 has been my "go to" Scripture: "Be joyful always; pray continually; give thanks in all circumstances, for this is God's will for you in Christ Jesus." This can be difficult. It is an act of obedience. Happiness is based on circumstances, but joy is eternal because God is with us. As long as we trust God, that inward joy is lasting.

Second Corinthians 12:8b says, "My grace is sufficient for you for my power is made perfect in weakness." God may not remove the problem, but His grace will increase. His power is more than enough and reveals itself when we have nothing left. From strength to strength His power will carry us through.

There were times when it felt as though God had His arms wrapped around me. His presence so near. It seemed as if I was breathing celestial air. An indescribable feeling that often times brought me to tears because I couldn't contain the emotion of His nearness.

To the world, I am no one special. I don't have a lot of letters behind my name. I'm not famous. I'm not wealthy in the world's eyes. I am a wife, mom, grandmother, sister, friend and teacher of God's Word. But to God, I am someone of enormous worth. I have become a part of His family. I am a child of God! All of this is promised to those who understand that we are all sinners and Jesus died on the cross for our sins and was resurrected by God the Father. Faith (believing) is the step between promise and assurance. There are two unchangeable things about God: His nature and His promises. God is good and trustworthy to those who believe Him.

We are on this earth such a short time. It is a blink of the eye compared to eternity. Eternal things are of Heaven.

God has a purpose and a plan for our lives while we are here on this earth. Wisdom seeks God and uses our days for His glory. The Word of God shows us the way to Heaven. Heaven became a reality when Lee went to be with the Lord. There is life after death. God's Word declares it. Paul tells us that as believers, our home is in Heaven. If you are not a believer, Scripture tells us you will be separated from God for eternity.

> *"Teach us to number our days aright, that we may gain a heart of wisdom" (Psalm 90:12).*

The angel told me that wonderful day that God had a great plan for my life. One of my greatest joys is teaching God's Word. He has filled my heart to overflowing and I just have to share what I have learned.

I cannot contain it! I now teach Sunday School and small groups on Wednesday nights. I had always wanted to teach. I just didn't know God had intended it to be His Word!

I came to write this book because I kept reading in Scripture in The Book of Psalms where David was so thankful to God that he promised to proclaim His deeds. That is the purpose of this book, to proclaim the deeds of God. To give Him all the glory! It has been my journey, but it most definitely has been God's story. His amazing story weaved throughout my life.

Do you have a story with Jesus? Share your journey walking with Him with others. Proclaim your story.

I Love To Tell The Story
Arabella K. Hankey
I love to tell the story of unseen things above,
Of Jesus and His glory, of Jesus and His love;
I love to tell the story, because I know 'tis true,
It satisfies my longings as nothing else can do.
I love to tell the story
'Twill be my theme in glory
To tell the old, old story
Of Jesus and His love."
I love to tell the story, more wonderful it seems
Than all the golden fancies of all our golden dreams;
I love to tell the story, it did so much for me,
And that is just the reason I tell it now to thee.
I love to tell the story, 'tis pleasant to repeat,
What seems each time I tell it more wonderfully sweet;
I love to tell the story, for some have never heard
The message of salvation from God's own holy Word.
I love to tell the story, for those who know it best
Seem hungering and thirsting to hear it like the rest;
And when in scenes of glory I sing the new, new song.
'Twill be the old, old story that I have loved so long. [8]

"Do you not know? Have you not heard? The Lord is the everlasting God, the Creator of the ends of the earth. He will not grow tired or weary, and his understanding no one can fathom. He gives strength to the weary and increases the power of the weak. Even youths grow tired and weary, and young men stumble and fall; but those who hope in the Lord will renew their strength. They will soar on wings like eagles; they will run and not grow weary, they will walk and not be faint" (Isaiah 40:28-31).

35. John and me with our new granddaughter.

36. Brad, me, Jenna, and John with our granddaughter at her christening.

37. John, me and our granddaughter at Christmas.

38. John and me celebrating our 40th wedding anniversary.

39. Brad, Jenna, our granddaughter and John 2020

TWELVE

Salvation

"But, brothers, I want to remind you of the gospel I preached
to you, which you received and on which you have taken your
stand. By this gospel you are saved, if you hold firmly to the
word I preached to you. Otherwise, you have believed in vain.
For what I received I passed on to you of first importance:
that Christ died for our sins according to the Scriptures,
that he was buried, that he was raised on the third day
according to the Scriptures."
1 Corinthians 15: 1-4

S alvation is the number one theme of the Bible. The plan of salvation is for all people.

"For all have sinned and fallen short of the glory of God."
(Romans 3: 23)

When Adam and Eve sinned against God (didn't believe), they
brought sin into the world. The first step of faith is seeing our need for
a Savior. We are all born sinners and have need of a Savior. This is the
message of the Gospel of Grace that we need to believe to be saved.

It's not how good we are as people. But believing God sent His only begotten Son to pay the penalty of sin. The wages of sin is death. This is an eternal death. Jesus left the Throne Room of Heaven because He loved us and paid our sin debt by dying on the cross. Hebrews tells us that without the shedding of blood, there is no forgiveness of sin and without faith there is no pleasing God.

Romans Road to Salvation -

Romans 3:23	Everyone has sinned.
Romans 6:23	The penalty for our sin is death.
Romans 5:8	Jesus Christ died for sin.
Romans 10:8-10	To be forgiven for our sin, we must believe and confess that Jesus is Lord. Salvation comes through Jesus Christ.
Romans 10:17	"…faith comes from hearing the message, and the message is heard through the word of Christ."

God seeks us. He is waiting for us to respond. God always gives us the choice with access and invitation. Faith (believing God) is access to God. His greatest gift is allowing us to know Him.

> *"I am the way, the truth and the life. No one comes to the Father except through Me" (John 14:6).*

All who would believe the Gospel (Jesus died for our sins; was buried; and resurrected) is unlimited in scope. All people everywhere may come to a knowledge of salvation. Let us invite everyone to come and experience the living God now. It is an open invitation until Christ returns. Christ's return is more than a doctrine, it is a promise!

May all come and accept the invitation to believe and receive the hope of eternal life with Christ Jesus.

> *"Guide me in your truth and teach me, for you are God my Savior, and my hope is in you all day long" (Psalm 25:5).*

Word from the Father and Thoughts from My Sticky Notes

Through my journey as I sat with Jesus, there were so many times when I heard Him whisper to me through His Word. The Scripture resonated through my spirit and sometimes it seemed as if the words were so loud I had to stay God's hand. God's holiness overwhelmed me.

So, I started writing the Scripture or message on yellow sticky notes. People are always asking about my sticky notes, which fill my Bible. I tell them they were my journey with Jesus. The Holy Spirit speaking to me with the words I needed to hear at the exact moment I needed to hear them! Sometimes it was words of encouragement. They were sometimes words of affirmation. Often, they were words of comfort. They would be words of direction when I was not sure where to go. There were words of healing at the darkest of my days. Most especially, they were words always helping me to know God better.

As I was preparing to write this book, I went back and read my notes on all these sticky notes. That was the first time I had sat down and looked at all these messages from God. So, I thought I would share them with you. We are so blessed to have a loving Father who knows our every need.

Psalm 36:9: "For with you is the fountain of life."

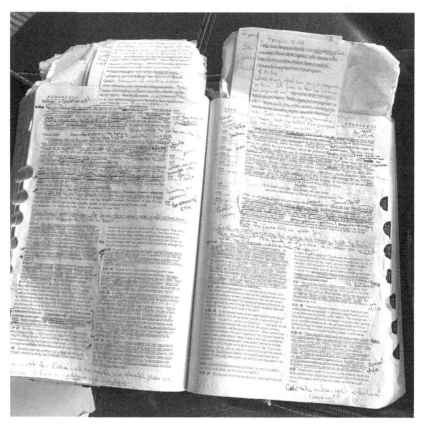

40. This is my Bible worn and full of sticky notes and written notes.

I heard God calling me after my treatments. I was going to jump in the fountain to refresh me. Quenching my spiritual thirst after being in the desert. Hearing God so clearly. Still so powerful.

To delight in the Lord means to experience great joy in His presence. It happens only when we know Him well.

Wait upon the Lord. He will make the next step clear.

Psalm 46:1, "God is our refuge, an ever present help in trouble."

A quiet confidence in God's ability to save us during difficult times.

Stand quietly before the Lord Almighty and be amazed. To see His power and majesty.

> Psalm 91:11, "For He will command His angels concerning you to guard you in all your ways."

Angels in Ingles told me I was beautiful.

As I daily crawled into Jesus' lap and took refuge.

Put God's Word to work in our lives, making it a vital guide for everything we do.

Keeping God's Word in my heart

> Proverbs 16:9, "In his heart a man plans his course, but the Lord declares his steps."

If you want to see God laugh, just tell him your plans.

God is in control and His plans are perfect. He knows from beginning to end.

> Isaiah 50:4b "He wakens me morning by morning, wakens my ear to listen like one being taught."

That's when I hear the Lord speak to me when I'm waking up early in the morning! Truly amazing!

> Jeremiah 29:11, "'For I know the plans I have for you,' declares the Lord, 'plans to prosper you and not to harm you, plans to give you hope and a future.'"

This is what the angel told me about God's plans for my life and that I was cancer free.

We can be confident in our relationship with God. It simply takes faith in God and a willingness to act on the faith.

Take your eyes off your troubles and look to God.

Zephaniah 3:17, "The Lord your God is with you, he is mighty to save. He will take great delight in you, He will quiet you with His love, He will rejoice over you with singing."

There were times when it felt as though God had His arms wrapped around me! His presence so near! It seemed as if I was breathing celestial air, an indescribable feeling.

Love lifted me.

Matthew 11:28, "Come to Me all who are weary and burdened and I will give you rest."

I found rest for my soul. In His rest is where I most often hear His sweet whispers deep within my soul.

Luke 1:37, "For nothing is impossible with God!"

Wait for the Lord and trust His timing.

We want to be in control. But when Lee came into our lives, we couldn't change his health issues. It was out of our control.

When God touches your life, you want to shout it from the mountaintop. It's so amazing you can't contain yourself.

Take advantage of the opportunities given to us doing what we can do and not worrying about what we cannot.

John 14:17, "The Spirit of truth. The world cannot accept him because it neither sees Him nor knows Him. But, you know Him for He lives with you and will be in you."
Third Person of the Trinity – The Holy Spirit.

The end result of the Holy Spirit's work in you is Christ's peace. Peace that transcends our understanding. A deep and lasting peace in the present and future.

Romans 5:5, "And hope does not disappoint, because God has poured out His love into our hearts by the Holy Spirit, whom He has given us."

During difficult times as we wait for God's will to unfold, we should place our trust in His goodness and wisdom.

Romans 8:28, "And we know that in all things God works for the good of those who love Him, who have been called according to His purpose."

Romans 12:12, "Be joyful in hope, patient in affliction and faithful in prayer."

2 Corinthians 1:3-4, "Praise be to the God and Father of our Lord Jesus Christ, The Father of compassion and the God of all comfort. Who comforts us in all our troubles, so that we can comfort those in any trouble with the comfort we ourselves have received from God."

2 Corinthians 1:8b-9 "We were under great pressure, far beyond our abilities to endure, so that we despaired even of life. Indeed, in our hearts we felt the sentence of death. But, this happened that we might not rely on ourselves, but on God, who raises the dead."

God is sufficient! His comfort includes receiving strength, encouragement, and hope to endure.

2 Corinthians 5:7, "We live by faith, not by sight".

2 Corinthians 12:8b, "My grace is sufficient for you for my power is made perfect in weakness. Therefore, I will boast all the more gladly about my weaknesses, so that Christ's power may rest on me".

Not removing the problem, but increasing the grace. His power is sufficient and shows itself when we have nothing left.

Ephesians 3:16-19, "I pray that out of his glorious riches he may strengthen you with power through his Spirit in your inner being, so that Christ may dwell in your hearts through faith. And I pray that you, being rooted, and established in love, may have power, together with all the saints to grasp how wide and long and high and deep is the love of Christ, and to know this love that surpasses knowledge, that you may be filled to the measure of all the fullness of God."

God's love is total.

Philippians 1:6, "Being confident of this that he who began a good work in you will carry it on until the day of Christ Jesus."

The day of Christ, the Rapture (catching away) of the Body of Christ

Philippians 4:4-7, "Rejoice in the Lord always. I will say it again: Rejoice! Let your gentleness be evident to all. The Lord is near. Do not be anxious about anything, but in everything, by prayer and petition, with thanksgiving, present your requests to God. And the peace of God, which transcends all understanding, will guard your hearts and your minds in Christ Jesus."

Philippians 4:11b-13, "For I have learned to be content whatever the circumstances. I know what it is to be in need, and

I know what it is to have plenty. I have learned the secret of being content in any and every situation, whether well fed or hungry, whether living in plenty or in want. I can do everything through him who gives me strength."

We can trust God will always meet our needs. Not necessarily our wants, but definitely our needs.

Colossians 4:2 "Devote yourselves to prayer, being watchful and thankful."

1 Thessalonians 5:16-18, "Be joyful always; pray continually; give thanks in all circumstances, for this is God's will for you in Christ Jesus."

2 Thessalonians 2:16-17, "May our Lord Jesus Christ himself and God our Father, who loved us and by his grace gave us eternal encouragement and good hope, encourage your hearts and strengthen you in every good deed and word."

2 Thessalonians 3:16, "Now may the Lord of peace himself give you peace at all times and in every way. The Lord be with all of you."

Christ's return is more than a doctrine, it is a promise.

2 Timothy 4:6-8, "For I am already being poured out like a drink offering, and the time has come for my departure. I have fought the good fight, I have finished the race, I have kept the faith. Now there is in store for me the crown of righteousness which the Lord, the righteous Judge, will award to me on that day - and not only to me, but also to all who have longed for his appearing."

Whatever we may face – discouragement, persecution, death; we know our reward is with Christ in Heaven.

> *Titus 1:2, "A faith and knowledge resting on the hope of eternal life, which God, who does not lie, promised before the beginning of time."*

It is the very nature of God to keep His promises!
The two unchangeable things about God – His nature and His promises. He is trustworthy and just.

> *Hebrews 6:18-19a, "God did this so that, by two unchangeable things, in which it is impossible for God to lie, we who have fled to take hold of the hope offered to us may be greatly encouraged. We have this hope as an anchor for the soul, firm and secure."*

Hope is the cord connecting us to heaven! Secure and immovable, anchored in God!

> *Hebrews 10:23, "Let us hold unswervingly to the hope we profess, for He who promised is faithful."*

> *Hebrews 11:1, "Now faith is being sure of what we hope for and certain of what we do not see."*

Believing God and His promises, I've found when seeking after God, I've experienced Him with His intimate presence.
True faith helps us see beyond the grave to eternal life in Heaven.

> *Hebrews 12:2a, "Let us fix our eyes on Jesus."*

Not to fix our eyes on our circumstances, but on Jesus.

As Christians, we should have a present-tense excitement, a soon anticipation of Heaven!

Hebrews 13:8, "Jesus Christ is the same yesterday, today and tomorrow."

We can trust our never changing Lord.

James 1:2, "Consider it pure joy, my brothers, whenever you face trials of many kinds, because you know that the testing of your faith develops perseverance. Perseverance must finish its work so that you may be mature and complete, not lacking anything."

Turn our hardships into times of learning. Not necessarily to be happy, but to have a good attitude. Waiting on the Lord, to be patient, to see what God will do in and through your circumstances.

James 4:10, "Humble yourselves before the Lord and He will lift you up."

Come near to God and He will come near to you.

1 Peter 1:8-9, " Though you have not seen Him, you love Him; and even though you do not see him now, you believe in him and are filled with an inexpressible and glorious joy, for you are receiving the goal of your faith, the salvation of your souls."

1 Peter 5:6, "Humble yourselves, therefore, under God's mighty hand, that He may lift you up in due time. Cast all your anxiety on Him because He cares for you."

2 Peter 1:2, "Grace and peace be yours in abundance through the knowledge of God and of Jesus our Lord."

The knowledge of God comes through Bible study and prayer.

1 John 4:19, "We love because he first loved us."

Notes

[1] Joni Eareckson Tada, *Diamonds In The Dust,* (Grand Rapids, Michigan: Zondervan, 1993), September 3

[2] James Rowe, "Love Lifted Me," (Saugatuk, Conn., 1912)

[3] Clara H. Scott, "Open My Eyes That I May See," published in *Best Hymns No. 2* by Elisha A. Hoffman & Harold F. Sayles (Chicago: Evangelical Publishing Company, 1895).

[4] Sarah Young, *Jesus Calling,* (Nashville, Tennessee: Thomas Nelson, 2004), 74

[5] Joni Eareckson Tada, *Diamonds In The Dust,* September 3

[6] Robin Schmidt, *101 Amazing Things About Heaven,* (Tulsa, Oklahoma: Bordon Books, 2004), 98

[7] Sarah Young, *Jesus Calling,* 370

[8] Arabella K. Hankey, "I Love To Tell The Story," published in *Joyful Songs* by William G. Fischer (Philadelphia: Methodist Episcopal Book Room, 1866).

Photo Credits